You are 14 years old,
your parents just left you in a foreign country:
illegal, no money, few family relations,
and in the 10th largest city in America.

You Have Been

LEFT iN AMERiCA

Left in America Organization
154 Glass St., Suite 108
Dallas, TX 75207
www.leftinamerica.org

HIS Publishing Group is a division of Human Improvement Specialists, llc. For information visit www.hispubg.com or contact publisher at info@hispubg.com

Library of Congress Number: 2015939769
ISBN-13: 978-0-578-16255-3

LEFT IN AMERICA
Summary: One young man's fight for life after being left alone by his parents in a foreign country.
—Provided by the publisher.

Printed in the United States of America

10 9 8 7 6 5 4 3 2
2nd Edition

LEFT iN AMERICA

THE STORY OF JUAN TERRAZAS

by SALLY SALAS

HISPUBLISHING GROUP

www.hispubg.com

A division of HISpecialists, llc

DEDICATION

I dedicate this book to my parents, Juan and Aurora Terrazas, my brothers, Luis and Isaac, and my sisters, Maria and Alma. Though separated for many years, a river of tears unites us. You are the reason I did not quit. I truly miss you, but I know the day is coming when we will be together again, so hold on. I love you, Ma and Pa. And to everyone who has loved me, and treated me like family along the way... there are not words enough to thank you.

—*Juan Terrazas*

To my children, to my students past and present, to all the immigrants who fill my life, may your lives make all that has gone before—the poverty, the pain, the struggles, and the sacrifices—be worth it in the end. May you not waste one minute of separation from family, country, or comfort on anything less than your best. May you dream big, work hard, learn much, and overcome! You have richly blessed my life.

—*Sally Salas*

Regardless of race, religion, or sex, this book is dedicated to the children living in America illegally, brought by parents seeking a better life. We believe these children deserve an education, the love of a family, and the opportunity to live free, productive lives in the only world they really know. It is our prayer that they find hope in this story.

—*Left in America Organization*

TABLE OF CONTENTS

ACKNOWLEDGMENTS

This book is the work of Left In America Organization (LIA). LIA Directors are Ed Blair (Managing Director), Lane Fleming, and Deborah Walker. Additional members of the Organization are Sally Salas (Author), Juan Terrazas, Scott Robson, Carolyn Strickfaden, Paul Zoltan LLP, and David Funke (Director of Dallas YWAM).

As Managing Director of LIA, I would like to thank all members of LIA for the long and dedicated work to this book.

We would especially like to thank Sally Salas for her work as the author of Juan's story. Without Sally's hard work and many hours of researching Juan's family members and friends, you would not be able to enjoy the beautiful story you are about to read. We appreciate the dedication it took to travel to Juarez without regard for danger to meet Juan's parents, in order to add depth and truth to places Juan's memory could not reach.

We would also like to thank Juan's family and friends for their time and for trusting Sally with their stories.

Specifically these family members

Juan Lorenzo Terrazas Pizarro and
Aurora Castillo Monroy (Father and Mother)

Alma Guadalupe Terrazas Castillo and Maria (Nena)
Elena Terrazas Castillo (Sisters),

Luis Donaldo Terrazas Castillo and
Isaac Josue Terrazas Castillo (Brothers)

Diana Gabriela Castillo Terrazas (Gabby) and
Diana Estefania Mota Castillo

Friends and people who are part of Juan's story:

Ricardo (Big Richie) Ramos

David Funke (Director of YWAM, Dallas) Emele Falahola
(YWAM Volunteer)

Joe Martin (Senior Pastor, Trinity Church Dallas)

Scott Robson, Dustin Sample, Carla Rivera, Ralph Rivera,
Sandra Ramos, Pastor Clay Wallace, Barbara Wallace,
James Musyoki, Crissy Robertson, Anthony McShan, Siti
Davis, Ricardo Ceballos (Tall Richie), Jesus (Jesse) Alanis,
Cesar Mota, Maria Meza Castillo (Tia Licha), and Cesar
Meza, Vincent Morelos, Carl & Cerrissa Trevino, Brian &
Carolyn Strickfaden and Amy Mulloy (Juan's Fiance)

ABOUT THE AUTHOR

SALLY SALAS WAS raised in the midst of Crossfire, an inner city ministry to youth in predominately Hispanic East Dallas, founded in 1990 by her mother. She grew up living among gangsters who began to meet Jesus, get off the streets, and change their lives. When she graduated from University of Houston with a Major in Creative Writing and Minor in Education, her great love for the inner city led her to teach in low income, Title I schools, where she has taught English, Reading, and English as a Second Language since 2000.

Sally is passionate about the written word, and about instilling confidence and self-worth in her students: watching them realize they are smart and capable, in charge of how hard they work and what they make of themselves. She fiercely loves and advocates for them, cheering them on long after they leave her classroom.

Juan and Sally working on the book.

FOREWORD

I WAS SITTING IN TRINITY CHURCH in Dallas with my wife Debbie when our Pastor began talking about members who volunteered. He mentioned a high school kid (Juan had actually just graduated from high school) who came on his own during the week to help around the building; vacuuming carpets, cleaning windows, dusting, and anything else that needed to be done. Pastor Joe Martin asked the young man to stand up, and I saw Juan for the first time: a tall, slender, young man with long hair.

I observed Juan in the weeks that followed, visiting, laughing, and praying with others. It amazed me that he was so young, yet a mature love for people just seemed to flow out of him. It was 2009, my wife Debbie and I were new to Trinity Church. Each Sunday, I introduced myself to people in the congregation, and as I talked with the members, I also asked about Juan. The answer always seemed to be the same: "That young man is the best! Always happy, always helping."

We also began attending a morning prayer group and had the opportunity on several occasions to be in a small group with David Funke, the Director of Youth With A Mission (YWAM) Dallas, the mission where Juan was living. We joined David in praying for his ministry, the financial and practical needs. In response to one need David shared, Debbie and I began dropping by YWAM Kids Club every week with desserts and drinks, briefly visiting with the children and adults before their sessions. During this time, I was able to get to know Juan. He was always there, helping in the kitchen, setting up chairs, and playing with kids as they arrived. I was able to watch him interacting with leaders and teaching young kids' Bible Study, always smiling, softly speaking to each child as if they were the only one in the room.

I saw Juan mature over the months and years, continuing to be amazed at his dedication to church, to YWAM, and to his education. One Sunday after church Debbie and Juan were visiting. Juan was talking about his life and how his music had become his way of communicating his journey. Debbie immediately heard a voice saying this story needs to be told. It's a story of those who are lost and find love and hope in Jesus Christ by developing faith in him and his chosen path.

Several Sundays later, Debbie and I had the privilege of listening while Juan told us the full version of how he came to live at YWAM. We sat in amazement; we couldn't imagine leaving a young boy of just 14 years old in another country. More than that, it was hard to believe that a young boy left on the streets of Dallas at such a young age, could turn out to be the fine young man we were having lunch with.

We could not get Juan's story out of our heads until one morning Debbie said, "You know, there should be a documentary about children who have been left in America after their parents are deported." We both realized Juan and his story should be told to others. I knew instantly that I might as well get to work. History has proven that my smart, creative wife has great ideas. My role is providing the foot work to help her make those ideas come alive. Almost immediately, we began to work on how to tell Juan's story.

During this process, my eyes were opened even more to how "normal" Juan's story is. After researching and talking to people, I realized how many children in America have similar stories. America needs to be challenged to do something about the children who have been left in America; Churches, Christian Organizations, and Christians have a choice to make. The plight of the children of illegal immigrants is a problem that isn't talked about or addressed and has no easy solution outside of the individual acts of love and care by Christians who love God and love people. What would have happened to Juan had he not met the Lord? If he had not met men and women who love God and love people? What will happen to all of the other children who have been left alone in America? It was this question that led us to forming the Left in America organization.

Left in America (LIA) is a Texas Non-Profit Organization officially formed in 2013, though work begun a year earlier, with the intention of writing and publishing the story of Juan Terrazas in order to inspire both immigrant children and Christians of America.

For this purpose, LIA has received contributions for expenses and operations. All funds raised to date have been used solely for that function. LIA will continue to promote and distribute the book Left in America, support the ministry of Juan Terrazas and YWAM Dallas.

LIA encourages churches, organizations, and individuals to become involved in supporting the work of organizations and individuals who care for and support children of illegal immigrants. We hope that you support these organizations not only financially, but also with prayer, volunteering your time and efforts, and getting to know these children personally. It will bless you more than you can imagine!

Blessings, **Ed Blair**
Managing Director LEFT IN AMERICA

LIA is a non-denominational Christian Organization dedicated to helping children who have been left in America. Individuals and organizations that wish to join or contribute may do so by contacting the address below.

LEFT IN AMERICA ORGANIZATION
154 Glass St., Suite 108
Dallas, TX 75207

Or contacting us through our web site:
www.leftinamerica.org

PART ONE
The Road out of Juárez
La Salida de Juárez

"I am not Mexican. I am not a gringo. I am not Chicano. I am not a gringo in the USA and Mexican in México. I am Chicano everywhere. I do not have to assimilate to anything. I have my own history."

—*Carlos Fuentes*

"Yo no soy Mexicano. Yo no soy gringo. Yo no soy chicano. No soy gringo en USA y mexicano en México. Soy chicano en todas partes. No tengo que asimilarme a nada. Tengo mi propia historia."

— *Carlos Fuentes*

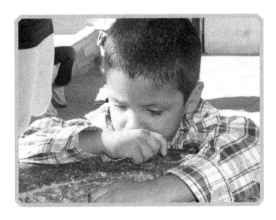

CHAPTER ONE

BY SALLY

Two Versions ... One Story
Dos Versiones... Una Historia

WHEN I GOT MARRIED, there were two versions of invitations to my wedding: one in Spanish and one in English. *Oh, how culturally sensitive of her*, you might think, but before you dole out too many accolades, it was really about cultural awareness more than sensitivity.

I didn't want anyone to have to wait.

You see, the Spanish invitation said 6:00 p.m., while the English invitation said 6:30. All of the non-Mexicans were seated, ready for the ceremony to begin at 6:15, but we held the service for the Mexicans, including my mother-in-law, who arrived at 6:50 carrying Spanish invitations. You know, the one that stated 6:00?

The wedding was outside under a beautiful tree by the lake, which meant there were no buildings around, so I hid in a van, sort of half sitting, half squatting in my wedding dress, waiting for my mother-in-law to arrive so we could begin.

I was totally, absolutely, not one bit surprised by her late arrival. I expected it, thus I prepared for it with two start times. I knew the culture. I grew up in the culture. And while some things about it, (like

3

the tendency to ignore clocks) can be irritating, I am actually much more comfortable with many parts of Mexican culture than with my own white, middle class beginnings of life. So much so, that just this week a middle school student of mine asked, "Miss... are you white? Or Mexican?"

Though not uncommon, it is quite a ridiculous question, for I have spent decades trying to shrug the nickname Casper, given due to my utter pastiness and prove to the world—and myself—that I can get a tan. Well, sort of.

But his question wasn't off base. Blonde hair and blue eyes aside, I bear a Spanish last name. Sally Salas. I teach English as a Second Language to middle school students whose first language is not English. I speak Spanish. Not well, mind you, but I can usually get by. I can tell you what to expect at a *Quinceañera*[1], what *menudo*[2] looks like when it's not hot (GROSS!), and what you should do if anyone gives you *ojo*[3]. So he's not the first kid who has wondered about my true ethnicity.

"Yes, *mijo*[4]," I answered him. "I'm white."

"Well then, how come you speak Spanish?"

"That, well, that is a very long story."

---

1 Coming of age celebration for a Hispanic girl on her 15th birthday.

2 *A traditional Mexican soup made of beef stomach and a red broth.*

3 A Hispanic superstition about someone giving 'the evil eye.' '*Me dio ojo*' – They gave me the evil eye.

4 Spanish term of endearment, combining '*mi*'– *my*, and '*hijo*'– *son*, i.e. '*my son*'.

CHAPTER TWO
BY JUAN

¡ Remember México
Recuerdo México

MY NAME IS Juan Antonio Terrazas Castillo, and I was born in Ciudad Juárez, México. Juárez is my home, I guess. At the least, it is my origin. Now known to the rest of the world as treacherous, drug-infested, and cryptic, it's probably the place that has made me the most who I am, though not in the ways you might think; it carved deeply into me and pierced through my skin to show itself. México identified me, branded me forever. Juárez formed my family out of the dirt and loud music of the city around it. It didn't just form brown skin or an accent, but also thought processes, poverty, and all of the ways that stretch life out before us like a road and show us where to go.

México has been that road, I suppose. The road my family has traveled in both directions. No matter which turns have been taken or busses hopped, it has lured us back. It haunts us. Everywhere else has just been a blur of downtown Dallas: up and down Ross Avenue, off of Ferguson Road, or a place I slept once, for a while. The others are places I have grown into, but México. México, I have had to grow out of, even though I don't remember much of it.

I do remember I loved boots. I had a pair of cowboy boots, not even sure where I got them or who gave them to me, but I know I loved them and wore them until I could no longer squeeze my feet inside. When they didn't fit any more, I just carried them everywhere I went. Pa called me *Vaquero*... Cowboy.

I remember in those early, fuzzy memories that are more like daydreams than something that actually happened, I was walking around with something in my mouth. I think it was a *peso*. I got on my sister Maria's nerves, and she hit me. In the swirling cloud memory, I swallowed the *peso*, and for years, that's where I thought my belly button came from.

Peso's plummeted in 1980's, in 1985 it was worth $.17, by 1986 $.08.

And I remember it snowed once in México. Can you believe that? Such a special moment. The grey and brown dirty desert of Juárez, mixed with crisp, clean, white snow, like it was trying to purify the city. Go figure.

I do not remember my eldest brother, buried underneath Juárez and at peace. He was my mother's son, not my father's, and would have been 10 years older than me. Now he watches us from Heaven, propped up on Papa God's knee. I do remember Maria, my sister, also born of another father. To us, she is called Nena, and she grins only slightly in the fear that whatever is putting the smile on her face could be ripped away, because it almost always has been. She looks like more of México, five years more of *la tierra*, than I do because she's five years older. She returned first. She never fit anywhere that was too far from Abuelo's side.

I am the first born of Juan Lorenzo Terrazas Pizarro, the eldest son. My family calls me Toño. Then there is Alma, *mi hermanita,* with less of home than me, but no less wisdom. Just two and a half years of *puro Español*, of dirt, of Juárez. Nena, Alma, and me. I remember we are from México.

And I remember leaving México. Sort of.

CHAPTER THREE

BY SALLY

My Culture
Mi Culture

B EFORE I OFFEND OR confuse anyone, I am in no way going to pretend or assert that my view or experiences are a complete picture of the Mexican people. I am speaking in generalizations about two cultures—the Mexican culture and the culture of poverty—and I am speaking out of a place that has seen these two cultures overlap. My point of view has been carved from 25 years of living around, living with, becoming family to, teaching, marrying and taking the namesake of Mexican people. Most of those I have shared life with have been immigrants or first generations to be born in the United States. Most have been plagued with poverty and need.

All of us are products of our upbringing, economic status, and religious affiliations, mixed up and stirred together to create the specific culture of our lives. So it is that I have been honored to know and become a part of a certain mixture of Mexican culture. In helping Juan remember and record his life story on paper, I was privileged to hear about how his own culture was created: Mexican, poverty, orphan, American, Christian. This is his story, but in telling it, I recognize slivers of culture that run through many American lives, including mine.

My mother used to cook family meals every night. We came home from school each day, sat at the same place with a snack, did our homework, and had dinner. Predictable. Normal. But when I was about eleven, through a series of very 'God' circumstances, my somewhat typical, white, middle class mother began an inner-city gang ministry in a violent, poverty ridden, hopeless plot of ground in East Dallas. Over the next few years, my family went from being fairly ordinary to being a sort of phenomenon, both to my friends, always wondering who all of the Mexican punks hanging around my house were, as well as to the gangsters who moved in and lived with us.

We moved into the ghetto, into the youth center in the heart of inner city Dallas. The boys we came to know, these gangsters meeting Jesus, thought we were crazy! They had spent most of their lives daydreaming about moving out of that ten-block radius. In their experience, those blocks produced nothing but drugs, dead ends, and premature death, yet there we were, living in their midst. My mother became like their mother, and they became family in every way you can imagine.

We ate together, lived together, fought over the bathroom, and defended one another. My boyfriends got threatening looks from tattooed guys who were introduced as my brothers. I got in trouble if my grades were too low, and my brothers got in trouble when Mom had to pick them up at the police station. Not exactly traditional, but it was family all the same.

Middle class got further away, as poverty and its ways became familiar to me. Street smarts grew on me like extra limbs I was learning to use as I began to notice, and then understand, the ways and reasons the boys carried themselves, handled situations, and viewed the world the way they did. *Tejano* music, spicy food, and the rhythm of the Mexican people became just as much a part of my life as high school football games, homecoming, and planning for college.

I had always wanted to teach and to write, and having seen the boys struggle with education, I knew when I graduated college (with about ten Mexican ex-gangsters and my family cheering me across the stage) I wanted to teach in the inner city. I had realized school wasn't as easy for everyone as it was for me. I had seen that, though immigrant parents cared deeply about education and giving their children better opportunities in theory, there was little understanding of public school systems, and they could offer little support for their children. Most had known no other life than labor and lack of resources, so wanting 'something better' for their children still didn't always result in what middle class expectations would call success.

My students quickly became grafted into my heart. Their lives and ways were familiar to me: full of struggle and promise, but having no idea what that promise meant or could actually look like. They knew I loved them, and they cared for me, shared their lives with me, and taught me just as much as I taught them.

There is much heartache, however, working in the inner city. You see lives full of potential, starving for change. You cheer them on so strongly you feel as if the veins will pop out of your eyeballs! And then they drop out of school. Or get pregnant at the age of 15. Or turn into the very thing they've tried so hard to escape. Then you do it all again with another kid, another class.

On the occasion you actually get to see fruit—a kid realizes they really are smart and it causes them to catch a vision for more, or they draw a line in the sand and say they want to be different, or they walk away from drugs and stay clean, or they graduate—it is glorious and worth it all. But those occasions with my students were bought with blood, sweat, tears, and time, lots of time. I always wondered just how much, if any, all of the effort truly impacted their future.

Then I married Jose, one of Mom's very first gangsters from years ago.

CHAPTER FOUR
BY JUAN

But i Don't Remember...
Pero No Recuerdo...

L ONG BEFORE THESE things I remember, both of my parents were born and raised in Juárez, *en el estado de Chihuahua,* in the state of Chihuahua, *en México.* Children of laborers, slaughterhouse workers, and maids, their lives were full of struggle and poverty. They say that Juárez has always been the same, though Mama says she remembers the 80s were more peaceful; people could trust others with confidence and walk around the streets at midnight or three in the morning enjoying the heartbeat of the city. Yes, corruption rumbled underground and touched everything around it even then, but the violence was easier to avoid for the normal city dweller simply trying to survive.

Everyone knew that trouble existed, but at night when the lights went out. So the slow, gradual climb of la *ciudad* up the hill of random violence, danger, and mistrust that brands the lives of all who live there today was not foreign or a surprise to any who grew up familiar with the streets.

Like my pa. Leaving school after fifth grade because there was no money to pay for it, he quickly grew accustomed to *la calle*. The streets. He was third in line of four children in his family, had no way to pay for education since even primary grades cost in Juárez, and they had little more than *frijoles* to eat much of the time. A life of hopeless struggle—never having enough of anything no matter how you dig, work, or claw, it has a way of producing addiction, and Pa was no different. Becoming a serious alcoholic at a young age, he would disappear for days at a time, binge drinking on the streets when he couldn't find work, leaving my grandmother sick with worry.

Aurora, my mother, was born into a family of eleven children. She had six sisters, four brothers, and a very strict, tired mother. After a show down with her mother (my grandmother), Ma stomped out of the house at age eleven, saying she couldn't live there anymore. She found refuge with her grandfather, who gently spoke to her about the way exhaustion and raising children with very little could take its toll, urging my mother to return home in an effort to mend the relationship. However, ten children to care for was already too many, and my *abuela* (grandmother) had washed her hands of Ma when she stormed out, so when she tried to return, she was not allowed to stay. From a very early age, Ma mostly cared for herself. She, too, received no education past the fifth grade.

My mother had a son at the age of fifteen, and Nena, my sister, was born three years later. When Nena was tiny, my mother's first-born developed a heart complication and passed away. It was then she was permitted back into my grandparents' home for the first time in years as she set on a path to mend the heartache of losing her son and being abandoned by Nena's father. Ma's father, *mi abuelo,* tended to Nena as if she were his own daughter. That bond lasted until *Abuelo* breathed his last breath; Nena found refuge with her grandfather, just as my mother had found refuge with hers. He was the only loving father figure Nena has ever really known.

Ma worked as a waitress and served drinks at a local bar, becoming close friends with Lupe, my father's sister. In the mean time, my father was in a lucky streak of work and labored from before the sun came up until very late at night. He began coming home to food waiting on the table—good food! Pork, heart, *tripas*. After several nights of eating very well, he asked my grandmother, 'where's all this food coming from?' *De la vecina*, she said. From the neighbor girl. Pa knew at that moment he wanted to meet this neighbor!

It was actually my *Tía Lupe* (my Dad's sister) who introduced my mother and father when Pa came into the bar one night. Afterwards, Pa would watch for her late at night next door. Ma used to sleep on the patio because it was so much cooler outside, and my dad would throw pebbles to get her attention. They began to spend time together, and at first my *abuela* was thrilled. Their growing bond caused Pa to straighten up and stay around the house, no longer disappearing into the endless fog of alcohol haze. *She* did not realize, however, how close my parents were becoming.

As they became more serious, *Abuela* changed her mind and disapproved of her son dating a woman with a child. In a somewhat Mexican tradition, the matriarch was ruthless in trying to hang on to her son. Extreme measures went into breaking them up, going so far as to invite my father's ex-girlfriends to dinner when the two lovebirds would be around. Though to this day my grandmother possesses fierce jealousy and a lack of acceptance toward Ma, I thank God she was unsuccessful at coming between them, for my parents began a family together, and I was born in 1990.

It is a family tale that my grandmother looked at me when I was first born and swore I wasn't my father's son, that I was half Black, in one last stab at wedging herself between my parents. But instead, Alma was born two years later, and the next generation of the Terrazas clan was in full swing.

Chihuahua, in 1990, the year I was born, was still the poorest state in México, and Juárez was the hub of cartel and corruption. My parents loved one another, and Pa stopped drinking for a while, but the white knuckling difficulty of trying to build a future in the midst of destruction seemed impossible, and Pa soon returned to self-medicating; his frustration and helplessness often manifesting as harshness and anger.

Juan Lorenzo Terrazas Pizarro, Juan's Father walking the street in Juarez.

You see, in Mexico, even work is political and corrupt. Because the economy is so poor, and the government is so twisted, each hard working, scraping the dirt laborer is stamped with an expiration date. Thirty year olds might as well be 70. At 35, you are automatically booted to the back of the line of people fighting for the very few jobs available, and it is almost unheard of for a 40-year-old to pick up work.

There was hardly any work in México; still isn't. *Nunca hay trabajo.* A young, strong man in Juárez *might* be able to scrounge two days a week, which would rake in a whopping ten or fifteen dollars, every dollar is fought for. My father, then still very young by most standards, was nearing 30 and thus was running out of options.

About that same time in 1994, Ma remembers realizing that women were disappearing more and more; she was afraid to go outside. Violence became a new kind of character on stage all of the time, in every scene. Where it used to be avoided by looking the other way or pretending it wasn't there lurking in the corner, robberies, carjacking, rape, and murder all became daily, normal occurrences and fears for everyone.

By November of 1995, more than 20 women had been found slain on the streets of Juárez that year alone. Their bodies were hidden in dark alleys near the plaza, behind shops, and tossed out with the trash. These women were becoming a worldwide news story—who were they? What kinds of crimes were being done to them before they died? More importantly, what kinds of criminals were doing them? There were too many to believe their deaths were random or unconnected. Was it the work of a cartel or of a religious cult? Those are questions still being asked today, for the body count of these women has reached over 400 in the past 15 years. But it began there, in my city, in the early days of my parents trying to build a family.

But I remember none of that.

CHAPTER FIVE
BY SALLY

This is not my Story
Esta no es mi Historia

THIS IS NOT my story, nor is it Jose's, so I will just say this: I had been familiar with Mexican culture, what it was to come from an immigrant family, the trials and strife specific to poverty, and how all of those things affected a particular group of people before I married Jose. They were not new to me. But when I said vows and married in to this clan, I tied myself to these struggles and blessings in a way I had not previously known.

Generational struggles specific to this culture are passed down like hair color and are now a part of my children's bloodline. I married someone who, though extremely smart, dropped out of school after eighth grade because his parents, who worked all night and slept all day, could offer no supervision and no support in school because they had no education themselves. They were working hard and simply trying to survive. Jose believed for years he would not live past the age of 21, and this mindset crippled his beliefs about himself, his vision for life, and his hope for the future. He was sober when we married, yet had already spent many years addicted, and angry over his father's addiction and anger. Sober or not, those things don't simply melt away.

I married a man who to this day fights against his own poverty mentality. Poverty is wicked and does not leave without a fight, digging its fingernails into every piece of flesh it can hang on to, screaming, "There will never be enough, and there will never be peace no matter what you do, so what's the point?"

Marrying Jose taught me these things, as well as what it's like to stand in line at INS—Immigration and Naturalization Services. I know the disrespect, the run around, and the endless hoops that come with trying to renew paperwork for legal residency status. The looks people give a Mexican who looks like a laborer or because they 'seem suspicious?' I have learned those looks and received them because I was with him. My children have grandparents who cannot speak to them in English. These things are all part of straddling two worlds, two cultures.

But I also get homemade tamales for holidays. I have spread *masa* on cornhusks in an attempt to make them myself, but I wasn't very good at it. My children have piñatas on their birthdays, we stay awake until midnight on Christmas Eve to open presents, and they can roll their 'R's. My children also possess that thing that Mexicans have— that resourcefulness. The ability to look at a mountain and think, *Sure. I could move that. I just need a chain, a truck, some good music, and a little bit of time.* The steady trudge that does not overwhelm; it just comes with assurance that they can work hard enough, figure it out, and overcome.

My children and I have inherited the most precious, wonderful things about Mexican, immigrant culture. We have also inherited the products of strife, the collateral damage of immigration, alcoholism, anger, poverty, and lack of education.

Like I said, though, this is not my story. It is not Jose's story or the story of my students. I say these things to paint a picture. I am intimately aware of poverty and its ways. I know the compli- cated fingers that touch every area of immigration. No matter your political affiliation, none of these things are easy issues. Whether you're discussing

welfare, how to ensure our nation's safety and secure its borders, education in low-income areas, or what rights to allow children who were brought here illegally as infants and are now adults, there are no quick fixes.

I believe, however, as Christians, that *"Religion that God our Father accepts as pure is this: to look after the widow and the orphan in their distress,"* (James 1:27), and to *"speak up for those who cannot speak for themselves,"* (Proverbs 31:8). I believe *this* should be *every* Christian's story.

So when a family friend approached me and mentioned wanting to tell Juan's story—the story of a child who found himself orphaned, the story of an immigrant, the story of a kid who came from an illegal, addicted, uneducated, angry, abusive, poor past, but was found and loved by other people, and a story of a young man who has found and loves the Lord, I laughed and said, "Yes, that is a story I believe I can help you tell."

CHAPTER SIX

BY JUAN

Leaving México
Salida de México

IN THOSE EARLY days of my family, I was an adventurous, cowboy boot wearing, four and a half year old, tromping around wild and free because the fear of the violence, (in worldwide news stories and investigations) the fear of no food, and no work did not belong to me. It belonged to the rest of the world as they watched the news about my home, where survival was marked by struggle and factory workers, and comfort and wealth were marked by the bloodthirsty drug cartel and corrupt government. But the terror and worry were not mine. I don't remember it.

They belonged to my father. They belonged to almost every father there, and like many fathers at that time, he had already worn out his welcome on the job scene and was nearing the age of being passed over for the few scraps of work that existed. He left our home for the United States in order to find work, provide food for his family, and hope for a better future.

Several family members had already moved to the United States, reporting the ease that came with available work. One of my dad's

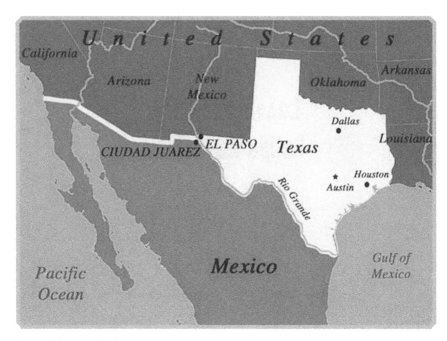

Map of Juarez - El Paso

brothers was working in Dallas and told Pa it should be relatively easy to make it to the El Paso airport and on to a plane with no immigration complications. Since an uncle on my mother's side also wanted to give the U.S. a try, the plan was to meet in El Paso and travel together. Pa said goodbye to all of us, went to El Paso, and waited, but my uncle never showed. He had chickened out, and my father was stuck there alone. My father who had never been anywhere but Juárez stuck out like a sore thumb wandering the airport. Immigration picked him up for looking suspicious, questioned him, fingerprinted him, and sent him back, but he had hidden his Mexican passport in his sock so they couldn't take it or have any information that would make it easier to track him.

After many phone calls and plans, he returned to the airport a week later under the direction of a *coyote,* someone hired to help smuggle illegals across the border. He was instructed to take a newspaper, sit in the lobby, and read it for a while without fear, like he belonged there. He was told to watch for a certain man to enter the restroom, then follow him. In the men's restroom, in the El Paso Airport, my father was handed a ticket to freedom. He folded it between the pages of the newspaper as he had been instructed and exited the bathroom with a grin on his face. The rest was easy.

He was in America, my home now, for about five months without us. In February of 1996, the rest of my family followed him. Back then, "the rest of us" was just me and the girls—mi Mama, Nena, Alma—and Ma's swollen belly. It cost my father $1,800 to send for us. He borrowed it from my uncle and can't even remember today if that paid a *coyote* or the expenses of his friends who drove to El Paso to pick us up, or who charged what. He just knew he wanted his family with him.

Most of what I remember about leaving México is very blurry. I have learned much more as an adult about the circumstances surrounding my snapshot memories, but in my childhood memory it was just Alma crying. I remember going, Alma and me, with another family and waiting in a hotel room and in a van with a lot of people, lots of children whining, complaining, messy, sticky, and hot. Alma was sobbing, and I thought that van ride to Dallas would never end.

Now I know that Ma sent Alma and me across the border with another family who claimed we were their children and used their children's papers so that we could cross 'legitimately,' safely. I now realize that Alma cried because we were with people who were not our parents. She didn't understand that my mother had taken Nena with her to search for another spot to cross the border to enter the United States.

Mama warned Nena to be super quiet, not one noise or rattle of the chains on the fence. *Silencio.* They could not draw attention to themselves. They were seen once and sent away. Ma says now that she spoke to a relative that day. *Tengo miedo.* "I'm afraid." He told Ma, "Just pray. Pray and ask for God's help." Ma prayed.

Later that evening, they took the advice of my *tío* and watched until the border was crowded. The line was full and the guards were busy, so they found a place that looked abandoned and safe to try again. Nena was silent and snuck through without a sound, but it

Juan, Nena, and Alma around the ages they came to America in 1996.

was my mother who, shaking and scared, hit the chains and rattled the fence. She has since told me her heart dropped, seized with terror. She froze, prayed, and looked straight at one of the guards. She can't believe to this day that no one saw her. They seemed to look straight at her, but turned and went the other way while Ma and Nena hurried in to safety, soon able to meet up with us and the family that helped carry us across.

That was the last night I ever laid eyes on México.

CHAPTER SEVEN
BY SALLY

Entering Juárez
Entrando a Juárez

I KNEW WHO JUAN was. Kind of. We had attended the same church off and on, and given my background, he's the kind of kid I would notice. Plus he's tall and has hair that... well, not many people have hair like him. It's like a Mexican Afro. I had seen him and his hair, but when I was asked to help write his story, I knew we would need to spend some serious time getting to know one another.

I'm sure it was nerve racking for him in the beginning. He was going to have to spill his guts: tell his most painful memories, dark things about his family, stories of strength and weakness to this random white lady he knew nothing about. But he quickly realized I was a trustworthy vessel for his story as he learned that the places he has trudged were places I knew something about.

We did run into the brick wall of his memory, though. So much of his formative years were hazy in his mind, which is to be expected, but unlike most, there are no connections close by he can call. There were no baby books, no pictures hung on walls to reflect his childhood back to him; there was no one to help him remember.

So I asked to go to Juárez.

I began researching the city that is known for its murder rate and dark alley scandals. In the past few years, Juárez has lost the title of most dangerous city in the world. Now it hovers somewhere around 6th place. Somehow, that news did not give my family much comfort, but that didn't register with me; I was excited, not afraid. I knew that in order to tell Juan's story, it was imperative to sit with his parents and read the emotions written on their faces when they spoke about their past and about leaving their children behind.

I needed to go. I wanted to go.

Juan, his sweet sister Alma, and his silly brother Luis, came to my house the night before I left. I snapped pictures of them to take with me to Juárez and watched them joke and wrestle with each other. Young adults who should be full of sadness filled my living room with laughter. They hugged me, told me to be careful and to have a good time.

"Is it hard knowing that I get to see them, and you don't?" The question I had been trying to hold on to spilled out.

Juan dropped his chin, grinned slightly, and cocked his head to the side. "No. I'm really happy you get to meet them."

"Is there anything I can bring back for you?"

"Tostadas and candy," he answered before I'd even finished asking the question.

Alma took a bit longer to answer. "I would really like a picture of them. That's it." She almost didn't get the words out without a few tears betraying her. They didn't fall though; they just sat on the edges of her eyelids.

I was leaving for Juárez, México, the next morning to meet their parents whom they hadn't seen in a decade, but they couldn't come with me.

As I boarded a plane to El Paso, the nervousness set in. Not about my personal safety, but about the possibly touchy situation I was walking in to. I was a white girl, walking across the borders of a country, across the threshold of a household with people who I have

Juan with sister Alma and brother Luis. This was the picture carried to Juarez by the author Sally Salas.

never met, to ask questions about a world I should not know. Juan Sr. and Aurora Terrazas did not know my background, and they did not know I was coming to get to know them, not to judge them.

I knew enough of Juan Sr.'s past to know he had a temper. My questions could ignite it because I needed to dig into intimate family details. I wrestled inside, worrying they may not open up or refuse to fill the holes in Juan's story. Or worse, become defensive, angry because I knew so many personal things they had not shared with me. I was very aware the meeting could go either way.

But as it turned out, I had nothing to worry about.

PART TWO
The Land of the Free
El País de la Libertad

"Give me your tired, your poor, Your huddled masses yearning to breathe free, The wretched refuse of your teeming shore. Send these, the homeless, tempest-tossed, to me: I lift my lamp beside the golden door."

—Emma Lazarus,
From the Poem on the Statue of Liberty

"Dame tus cansados, tus pobres, Tus masas amontonadas gimiendo por respirar libres, Los despreciados de tus congestionadas costas. Enviadme a estos, los desposeídos, basura de la tempestad. Levanto mi lámpara al lado de la puerta dorada."

—Emma Lazarus,
De la Poema engravado en la Statua de Libertad

CHAPTER EIGHT
BY JUAN

The Land of the Free
El País de la Libertad

SOMETHING STRIKES ME as strange, almost eerie, now that I have been back near the border as a young adult, the place where you can see both countries at once. Juárez is kind of like a sister-city to El Paso right across the border. You can stand on the U.S. side and see the flags flying, the gates and checkpoints, and guards. It is as if Juárez looms in the shadows of freedom in the back pocket of opportunity. In Juárez,, children who grow up and don't come to America as I did become increasingly aware with age that they could literally throw a rock and hit the land of the free and home of the brave. But they can't touch it. A place so near and yet so, so far and different. The crime, corruption, and poverty cease at that imaginary line. Even the air you breathe is different, hopelessness being sucked in on the Juárez side, yet opportunity in every nostril on the U.S. side. It is strange and something else I'm not sure what to make of yet.

The first thing I remember seeing in America on this side of that imaginary line was a plane—huge, sprawling, hanging in the air. I have no idea where or why, but it stuck in my head as an event. When I am asked about my memories of arriving home to my country, my people now, that plane is the first image in my mind. Symbolic, perhaps. Freedom? Perspective? Opportunity to see new places and things I would not have had the worldview to see in the poverty and corruption of Juárez? I am still young for my reflections to be complete. I'm still working some of these things out with the Lord. Nevertheless, this plane was probably in El Paso, for that's where we entered the United States, and there's a huge airport there. I remember gawking at it with my mouth open and my head all the way back in that way that makes your neck and throat hurt at the same time. I was so amazed. I had never seen a plane before.

When we arrived in Dallas, it was snowing. I'd only seen snow that one weird time back home. Dad chewed his nails to the nub, nervously waiting and then searching for someone who could drive him across town in the snow late at night. Many had told Pa to forget about us. "Find a woman here who could help you fix your papers. Marry her." It wasn't as if that never happened. Dad knew many who came in search of a better life for their families, never to return. He knew he could never do that; could never leave us behind.

And so, right around Valentine's Day, in 1996, in the middle of a rare Texas snowstorm, my family was reunited. Unlike the time it snowed in México and turned everything to a grayish, brownish sludge, the ground in Dallas shimmered white as Pa climbed out of a car and ran across the parking lot to embrace us. The snow fell as if to purify, washing away all of the dirt from Juárez from our lives and make them new. Pa looked proud as he welcomed us to new life.

A la nueva Vida. To this side of the border where the air felt different.

CHAPTER NINE
BY JUAN

My Father
Mi Pa

THE EARLIEST MEMORY I have of my father was in México, of course. We lived in a building, in a neighborhood I guess, not enough auto focus to call the snapshot into clarity or describe it, but I know we all lived in one room, in one bed, and the bathroom and shower were outside.

I was two or three years old, and there was a party, which with Mexicans, is all of the time. It was *toda familia*. Everyone there was family, mostly from my mom's side. Several of my *tíos*, mom's brothers, were holding my drunk, raging father down in a chair as he cursed and contorted, attempting to get loose from their grip. He was always unstoppable once he became angry, but they were sure trying. Then the memory jumps, arriving home to him already passed out asleep, having been carried or sent home ahead of us. As we all tried to climb into bed, I heard my mother urging him, *Muevete. Muevete.* "Scoot over. Scoot over." She nudged and rolled and pushed him over so we could all fit.

That's it. Nothing dramatic that would give reason for this episode to remain in the recesses of childhood remembrances. But there it is. Rage and then peace, as if it were on repeat as normal. I'm sure now that it was.

My father was physically and verbally abusive to all of us; mostly to Ma. He was always easily angered, seemingly out of nowhere. There was not any particular button to be avoided, or room to stay out of, or subject to dodge in order to control the explosions. We would have discovered a way to tiptoe around them had one existed. They were simply there, hanging in the air as an ominous presence in our lives that may or may not show up that day.

But he wasn't all bad. He was such a hard worker. He taught himself how to do anything, everything. He's been a mechanic, a builder, an electrician, and fixed things around our house (and everyone else's); anything you could think to put your hands to, he would find a way. He is the kind of jack-of-all-trades that poverty demands many become.

Mexicans are a resourceful, strong, sad, hardworking people. Betrayed by our own government and country, we are a people who have become self-reliant problem solvers, suspicious of most things and most people. My father is a clear manifestation of each of these qualities. I always thought of him as mysterious and wonderful; I thought he could do anything, and I wanted to be just like him. I would find things and try to fix them in attempt to mirror him: resourceful, strong, and proud.

He used to call me *Campeón,* Champion. When I was three or four years old, he would say, 'Let's race.' And I would run my heart out to the finish line to hear him say, *¡Ay, Campeón, me ganaste otra vez!* 'You beat me, again!' Then he would rub my head and leave for work, when he had work.

When I was a little older, he had a job driving a bus for a little while. I guess a school bus. There was a day when the whole family—cousins, *Tías,* all of us—loaded up on that bus and drove to a swimming hole type of place that had a bunch of pools and diving boards.

There were coolers, *comida*, drinks, all of it. It was a great day, one filled with peace. Then dad drove us all home again on the big bus.

There were good family times. But then that fun, resourceful, jack-of-all-trades would disappear and this other mysterious and scary part of the man we knew as Pa took his place. This other side of Pa was the suspicious, betrayed, angry part of the Mexican people; the side of Pa filled with rage.

Thankfully, I don't remember a lot of what my dad did to me, not even when I got older and we moved to the States. I just mostly remember the feeling of growing up afraid of my father. Yes, the overwhelming sensation was definitely fear. I recall being around nine or ten and talking to my mom about being scared of my dad. She said, "*Mijo*, this is not a good kind of fear." I'm not sure now if she meant that as an accusation toward me, as if to say 'fix it,' or an ache in her voice that wanted to scoop me up, protect me, and tell me there was nothing to be afraid of. But that was all she said, because there were no solutions.

A few years after that, I broke my arm. I had a cast and everything. Dad was in the midst of one of his grandiose explosions, screaming and verbally abusing Ma in front of me. I heard him hurl one of his usual lines at her: *la rata con dos patas.* 'You're just a rat on two feet.'

I was at the delicate edge of an age. Balancing between child and adult, I was a teenager old enough to be aware of my own anger, and of rage as I watched my father treat my mother harshly again, I began daydreaming of stepping up to him. Standing there holding my cast, I thought, 'How am I supposed to fight him with this thing?' I even imagined myself smashing my casted arm on the counter, re-breaking it, just to shock him into leaving Ma alone. But I just stood there, trembling with rage. I was at the edge of this age, not yet a man. Frozen. There was nothing I could do. It was one of the worst feelings of my life.

Then there were the times it was me he got rough with and not Ma. One day I stood, detached from the moment; he was hitting me and I thought, "Why is he doing this? I'm old enough now that it's not going to change who I am or what kind of man I'm going to be. Why is he hitting me if it's not going to change anything?" I had hardly any fear because anger had introduced itself to me and excused most of the fear from the table. I was bigger and he couldn't physically hurt me as much, so I wondered what he thought he would accomplish. Why did he continue to lay his hands on me since, in the Mexican culture, I was nearing the age of being a man? Later I talked with Ma about it all. "Doesn't he realize it has no effect on me? He's not going to change me."

I don't know for sure, but I imagine she told him about our conversation because we didn't have much time together after that, maybe only two years, but for those two years he never laid a hand on me again. *El nunca me tocó otra vez.*

CHAPTER TEN
BY JUAN

Early Days in America
Primeros Días en América

THE FIRST PLACE we lived when we moved to Dallas, long before the day my father chose not to lay a hand on me again, was Crystal Lake Apartments on Ferguson Street. Then there was the brick house on Petain Avenue. To us, it may as well have been a towering mansion with white, spiraling columns. It was a home. Brick! Violence on the streets like we knew it in Juárez was gone, there was work to be found—hard work that made my parents tired, but paid them for their efforts, and there was the difference in the air of promise, of opportunity. The air in Juárez did not have that.

One of my parents' jobs when we first came to Dallas was cleaning up a movie theatre. I suppose it was right upon our arrival because Luis was not born yet. At least, he is not present in these memories, but he could have been an infant. Nena, Alma, and I would go with them late at night and help. Well, sometimes we would help. Sometimes, we would curl up in the corner with blankets and sleep while Ma and Pa cleaned. I'm sure it wasn't fun for them. I'm sure it was hard work, but it was work. And they got paid for it, and our family was together and had hope. And we always left with a big bag of popcorn!

Those two early places, these homes, marked the happiest times in my family. We had cookouts every weekend, we went to church as a family, and I even remember my parents dancing together in that brick house.

My dad had met a man he worked for before we even arrived in the States who had invited him to church. Pa was hesitant and didn't want to go, but he worked for the man and didn't want to offend him, so he said yes. After visiting and feeling the presence of God, my dad began attending church and became committed to changing himself and our family. Pa had called home before we joined him in Dallas, telling Ma, 'No more partying. I want to be better. We're going to church, we are going to change.'

When my father first left México and promised to send for us, a large part of my mother's family thought he was gone forever. They knew his anger, his abuse, and his ways. They assumed he would leave, get involved with some other woman, and we would never see him again. They thought the worst. Expecting the worst was the kind of life they had in the years leading up to leaving México. Struggle and strife takes a lot out of a man, and my father had not known hope for many years.

So this man he worked with spoke of hope. He spoke of Jesus, and the heart of my father—part of who I know him to be, that longed to be a better man, a better father, better husband—opened up to hope. Pa stood up straight and declared to his family that things were changing; we were all going to church and following God. Ma could hardly believe him; she thought he had gone crazy. At first, she even resented what Pa was saying, "Of all the times I begged you to quit drinking, said I wanted to change, to get better, and you ignored me. Now I'm supposed to change because you say?" ¡Estas loco!

But they did. They quit drinking, and we all went to church as a family... for a while. My parents even got married! They had never been married before. The pastor of the church we were attending taught them about biblical marriage, and they wanted to follow God's plan for their lives, so I was at my parents' wedding as a five year old!

I believe that my parents' wedding was God ordained, planting Himself into the core of *mi familia* and shifting the eternal destiny of my siblings and me. It didn't mean much to us at the time because we were so young, and church was so new to my parents that they didn't know how to lead us spiritually. It wasn't until many years later that I watered that planting in my own life, and although not every member of my family claims or clings to the Lord today, His name was etched into our family tree a long time ago. I see that now.

CHAPTER ELEVEN
BY JUAN

Barriers
Barreras

L UIS WAS BORN shortly after we arrived in the United States and became the first division in *la familia*. He was a citizen of America; we were not. Then Isaac was born soon after, a citizen as well. *Americano*. I remember going to the hospital when Isaac was born to see him, seeing Ma and my sisters staring at him, and thinking his ears were strangely hairy. *Orejas peludas*. Those hairy ears divided us in half, tipping the scale a bit from those of us who remembered México.

In those early years in the States, our family grew and I began school. There was a struggle to learn English, I suppose, but I was so young it disappeared quickly and the language began to stick. I carry only a few scars from *la idioma*, my early language barrier.

In first grade, a little girl sat behind me. Isn't it always a girl who scars boys' memories? She constantly poked me in the back. To this day, I have no idea why she was really poking me. She may have been asking a question or trying to get my attention or picking on me on purpose, but in my first grade mind, she was stabbing me out of an evil, twisted heart. It hurt, and tears dangled at the edges of my eyes from the pain. But I had no words, no language, to ask for help, to tell her to stop, or report her to the teacher. The little girl poking me makes me mad all over again! But back then I learned to keep to myself, suck it up, get over it, and be all right.

Then one day a teacher gave me some papers to be delivered. Just like all kids that age and stage, I was proud to be chosen, trusted, and set apart. Trouble was, I had no idea what she asked me to do with them, no idea where the room was she had directed me to, and no vocabulary to figure it out. I wandered for a bit to appear gone from the classroom for what I assumed would be an appropriate amount of time, and then dropped the papers in the grass behind the portables. I sure hope they weren't important!

Those are the kinds of experiences that cause me to say México carved itself into me, that Juárez made me who I am. After all these years, I no longer feel Mexican. I barely remember México and now consider myself American. But I had to grow out of México and into the language, into the culture, into the hope of being American. I have trained myself to speak well, to sound educated. I laugh at a few of my family members; they still sound so... so... *Mexican!*

Even as I tease them, I remember the barriers that stood between others and me, how hard it was to not be equal for a number of reasons. These scars showed me what it is like not to belong. I no longer belong in México, my native origin; I would stick out like a sore thumb. But there are still those who say I don't belong here.

Because there have been countless moments in my life when I felt I belonged nowhere, that I had no home, nowhere to go or sleep or rest, I have learned what it means to be a stranger and an alien, to be *not of this land* [5]. Therefore, these scars, and others, are precious to me. Juárez taught me to grow out of this place and into Heaven. It was all for good.

It just didn't feel like it then.

---

5   5 I Peter 2: 11–12

CHAPTER TWELVE

BY JUAN

Doorways
Los Portales

WHEN I WAS ABOUT 10 years old, and that season of homes and happiness was drawing to a close, some people knocked on our door at Fairway Crossing apartments where we lived and invited us to come do this 'kids camp thing.' By that time, my older sister Nena was 15 and almost always hanging out with her friends. She was definitely too cool to be around Alma and me. She was a troublemaker, *traviesa,* mainly because Pa had begun to slip back into his old ways, being rough with Ma and slowly drinking again. Nena chose times such as these to remember that he was not her biological father. She was suspicious of him long before the rest of us knew we should be.

Isaac wasn't born yet, and Luis was a toddler—much too little to leave Ma's side, so just Alma and I went to this kids camp thing, now known to us as Vacation Bible School, for the promise of kickball and friends. We got just that. Arts and crafts, soccer, kids playing, and snacks! I was so lost in all of the excitement, I had no idea it had anything to do with Christianity or God. I was just having fun.

I had no idea that in the midst of all that fun, things that had been planted in me during those early times of going to church with my parents were being watered. I didn't know these things would eventually change me forever, and I didn't realize at first that John 3:16, *"For God so loved the world that He gave His only son,"* meant the Son was *given* for me and that I would one day not only believe in Him, but cling to Him. We had gone to church off and on since our arrival in the States and Pa's pronouncement that things would be different, but it was all so new. I had been so little, and the church going hadn't lasted long, so I never grasped the true Gospel or the love of Jesus.

However, at the end of that week of Vacation Bible School, I remember a teenage girl sitting down with Alma and me and asking if we had ever said a prayer to accept Jesus. We said no, so she led us through a prayer asking God to forgive our sin and asking Jesus to live in our hearts. I didn't really understand, and surely didn't realize the weight of that moment in my life, but I knew these were good, nice people, and I felt good when I was around them. I don't know where that grown up teenage girl is today, and I have no idea what her name was, but my prayer is that the Lord has honored her obedience and service and that she has been blessed richly for leading my sister and me to the Lord. She forever changed the destiny of our lives.

Don't get me wrong. Nothing much changed in the natural every day behavior of my life at that point. I was still a squirrely ten-year-old kid who liked to be wild and cause trouble, just like I had been at seven or eight, when I called 911 as a joke and hung up. Ma and Pa had gone to the store and left us alone for about 15 minutes. I phoned in my prank, not realizing of course that my number and location would be traced. The phone rang a minute after I hung up and Nena answered, assuring the operator that it must be some mistake, that everyone was fine. But by the time my parents came home, the police were there questioning us to ensure we weren't being held hostage.

So I was still a very typical kid, but I knew these people were different, and I knew I wanted to be different around them. The Lord had entered my life in a way I did not yet understand. A year later, when I was 11, I met David Funke of YWAM Dallas, a man who would water these seeds and see them grow.

David Funke, Director & Founder of YWAM Dallas.

CHAPTER THIRTEEN

BY JUAN

David

I WAS ELEVEN YEARS old the first time I laid eyes on David Funke, a huge, gentle man. He was the YWAM (Youth With A Mission) Dallas founder and director, though that meant nothing to me then, and I had no idea at the time how instrumental he would be in my life.

As is the custom in inner city, low-income apartments, I spent most of my days grubbing around outside with the neighborhood kids, but on Fridays, this white man would show up, and half the kids disappeared. Missing my friends was annoying. I knew it had something to do with 'churchy business,' but that was about all I knew. David says I was small, skinny, and shy and seemed to want nothing to do with him at first. He's probably right 'cause he interrupted my playtime!

After a while, though, and several invitations from friends, but probably mostly out of boredom, I decided to check out 'this churchy business' and go with them. David came to the door of our apartment with me, so I could point to him when asking Ma if I could go to church with the *gringo*. I registered a slight moment of embarrassment, glancing around with David looking on, and wondered what he thought about the tiny apartment space with little furniture, just a chair in the corner with a TV on it and five people sitting around on a bare floor, watching it. That was the year 2000, and ever since, he has been a fixture, like a piece of furniture, always there, in some corner of my life.

For several years, David, Kids Club, and YWAM were just options of places to go, things to do: entertainment, snacks, and distraction. I floated in an out of David's circle, if what he offered was better than anything else going on at the time, but he never seemed to mind. He is the most steady, laid back, constant, faithful human being I have ever come in contact with, yet it still took me a long time to trust him and his motives. One summer, he invited me to Kids Across America Camp in Missouri. I had never had the chance to do anything like that and was excited. Looking back now, I'm sure it was a huge amount of effort and a big hassle to get all of those off-the-radar, ghetto kids to fill out the necessary paperwork, make a plan, and return all the forms signed. It makes me laugh thinking about how different that is from what I've come to know as middle class, or normal, ways of operating.

The night before we left, David came by to make sure everything was good and that I was ready. I stared at the ground, kicking dirt around in a circle. "Mister... I can't go." I was humiliated, but in his gentle way, David nudged me with enough questions that I finally admitted the real reason. "I don't have any clothes to take." Apparently, the humiliation wasn't necessary because before I knew what was happening, we were in line at Wal-Mart, checking out with a week's worth of socks, t-shirts, and camp shorts, as well as all the toiletries a stinky, young teenage boy needs to make it through a week at sports camp. This is how life was with David. Faithful. Understated. Providing opportunities I would never have had otherwise, but never making a big deal about them.

I know now that David didn't start out in ministry. He did grow up in church, though. "Mama did the sangin, and Daddy did the teachin," he's told me. They didn't talk about Jesus, needy people, or God having a call on anyone's life and a job for them to do. "Nobody ever talked about stuff like that. Or if they did, I wasn't listening."

Public schools in David's hometown were desegregated when he was in the third grade, but in his world it didn't matter because there wasn't anyone who didn't look like him for miles and miles around. He didn't see a black or brown person with his very own eyes until the age of twelve, which is ironic, considering that in his daily life today, he's pretty much the minority. He had a nice, quiet life with no major tragedy, went to church on Sundays, and went to work in the steel mills of East Texas, having no interest in a career working with people. "I much preferred to work with machines. They behave. But I guess God had other plans," he laughed.

On a long break in 1986, he went to a weekend mission festival with YWAM to hear some Christian music groups in concert, and in a way only God can design, he ended up on a mission trip to México within a week. They did street ministry, just loving on and feeding people, and then spent a lot of time in an orphanage. Having never been exposed to Spanish, he could hardly communicate with anyone. "I mean, I didn't even know what 'hola' meant." But he realized words didn't even matter. The kids wanted hugs and attention. He had never seen the world as a needy place before and certainly hadn't thought that he had anything to offer. Realizing he needed no special gifts, no audible voice from God to know what to do or be able to help, and grasping the reality that all he had to do was to show up, David realized that being there could change people's lives, and that ruined him forever. Gripped by the desperate need of others and the deep compassion of God, he has never been the same since.

Not even wanting to return to work, but not knowing what else to do, David went back to his normal routine for about four weeks. "It was awful. All I could think about were the kids' faces, and how much need there was in the world." The Lord was so in charge of orchestrating the events of his life. The oil field industry crashed soon after he returned from his trip to México, and hundreds of layoffs were on the horizon. He had earned so much favor in the workplace that his supervisor called him in.

Juan & David, at YWAM Dallas Christmas program, 2010

"I sense that you're restless. You're not my choice for lay off, but if you want to go, I'll let you. It's much better for you financially if you're laid off than if you quit."

David says he felt like the Lord was asking, "What do you want to do, son? Do you want to stay here, in this life, or go on an adventure with me?"

So he went.

He has been a full time missionary to inner city America ever since, moving to Dallas with a team in 1992 to set up YWAM in the projects near downtown. They were given a piece of property, an extremely run down piece of property, next to a major drug dealer on the rough streets of East Dallas. They had no agenda except to be good neighbors, help clean the streets, and wait for the Lord to put something in front of them. What they saw in front of them, in every direction wherever they went, were needy children. Van loads of them.

I started jumping in David's van on Mondays, Fridays, summer camps way back when I was eleven years old. Sometimes, I was with him several times a week; sometimes, I'd go months without seeing

Juan translating for David Funke at a YWAM Dallas Christmas program, 2013

him. He never pushed me to be anywhere spiritually except for where I was. In fact, I'm sure there were years he wondered if he would ever see any fruit at all from the effort he poured into all us kids' lives. But not knowing never stopped him. Though it took years for me to see the big picture, grab hold of God on my own and not let go, when I look back on those years and remember milestones in my life—in the natural and in the spiritual—good ole faithful David was there, a fixture in my memory: taking me to camp, on mission trips, teaching, challenging, and loving me. He introduced me to the idea of the spiritual family, church family, that I could belong somewhere and that people could be responsible for me, even if I wasn't a blood relative. He introduced me to other men like him: Dustin Sample, the Youth Minister at Trinity Church, and Scott Robson, a strong, Christian father figure. Both would come to teach me things, father me, and walk beside me. No matter what happened, David was always there, coming to pick me up in a van and driving me further and further into the love of God.

CHAPTER FOURTEEN
BY JUAN

Storms
Las Tormentas

THE SEASON OF family life, this season of happiness, lasted until we moved to East Dallas. A cloud foreboding the storm that was to come seemed to move in with us. It happened so slowly though, no one realized it was getting dark. No one knew it was a warning.

Pa had moved through jobs and up the pay ladder, even reaching top cook at a restaurant at one point, and then found more money in construction. Construction led him to handy man jobs for a wealthy individual who was always asking him to come in and fix this or add that. Through observation, taking in the type of people that were always in and out of the man's fancy house and the inexplicable money rolling in, Pa figured he was a drug dealer, but never asked questions, for he was being paid to do a job. There were also 'perks.' There were always people at this big house, drinking, smoking, and enjoying their spoils. When Pa finished whatever odd job he'd been hired to do, they were there offering him a drink of this or a puff of that after a hard day's work.

He had also begun hanging out with my uncles more, and they were always happy to put a beer into his hand. Drinking quickly took hold of him once more as it had before we escaped the hopelessness of Juárez. This wealthy man who hired Pa slowly lured him into working more and more 'inside' jobs, finally asking him to come on full time and began having him work 'security.' Pa even took a few out of town trips with him. He was pretty sure they were moving drugs, but never asked, so that he could never be held accountable for knowing.

Between Pa's drinking and mild drug use, added to his new crowd of 'friends,' he and Ma had plenty to fight about.

It was somewhere around fifth grade when life began to change for the worse. My parents stopped going to church. Funny thing, though, we kids never really did. We soon became familiar with a neighborhood ministry group called YWAM. I knew David Funke and a few others from the local church Dallas Metro. I knew they were Christians, nice people, and I would go to hang out with the kids. Well, that and because Alma would make me go. She tried to make every-body go to Sunday School, VBS, everything. She would throw out a lasso and drag along anyone who came within the circle of where it fell. Even then, her heart was tender to the Lord.

Unfortunately, my heart was not always so tender toward her. In those days, Alma, being my closest sibling in age, was the one who bore the brunt of my bad attitude. She annoyed me constantly, and being older, I exercised my power through harsh words, hitting her, thundering at her, and lashing out. I did anything I could to get her to leave me alone. *Déjame en paz.* Probably because the mood in the house was changing, the clouds hanging lower and thicker, I spent most of my time away, wandering the neighborhood with my friends, playing, being a boy on the verge of making trouble. And my parents gave me the freedom to go unsupervised. I was hardly ever in the apartment, but when I was, I was arguing with Alma.

I argued with Alma, Pa argued with Ma, and the peaceful season we had all once enjoyed screeched to a halt. The storms were rolling in, though I wasn't really aware of it at the time. Alma says I didn't pay enough attention when we were younger, or I would have noticed what was happening. When she explains it now, it all sounds so familiar and I remember, even though I didn't see our family changing then.

The weekdays were a normal routine for all of us: work or school, play outside, come in for dinner, repeat. Then the weekend came. Ma and Pa would party with my *tíos* and with dad's new crowd of friends, and we would be along for the ride, hanging out with all of the other kids in the family and neighborhood while the parents drank and did drugs. The drugs are part of what I didn't realize then. I don't remember being aware of them. But I was aware that my parents would fight. Dad would get drunk and angry. Tension would increase all weekend until something would give, and the thunder of his temper ripped through the house. Through all of us.

The tension in our home became the new normal. We didn't know any different, for this same pattern played itself out in most of the families we saw around us. With the exception of Pa's anger, I thought life was all right. Wandering the streets as much as I did and being out of the house, I guess I missed the little clues that Alma seemed to pick up on.

The heavy verbal abuse didn't feel right in the air around my skin, but it wasn't necessarily wrong, either; it just was. It got to the point one day that Pa physically attacked Ma. I wasn't home, but Alma told me about it later. She said the room looked like a scene from a movie, moving in slow motion: Pa with his hand around Ma's throat and my little brothers, Alma, everyone screaming. Ma had only done what we all wanted to do hundreds of times; she had hid the bottle from him. That was all it took to make him explode.

Even then, those were just moments. Snapshots. It wasn't like that all of the time, and it wasn't as if all of life was bad. Pa had worked hard to give us all a better life. Parties were just part of that life, a time to let off steam and have fun. They were simply the way of the weekends, the way of a people who worked hard, struggled, but had managed to have the strength to make a way out of México, a place that had no work and offered nothing.

I thought my parents were simply coping with living away from their land and letting the stains from hard work ooze out of their pores. Their life style didn't need to make sense to me, and now that it does, no blame or grudge exists in the way they did things or in the road they took. It was the road out of México. But it was a road laced with storms, and it led Pa right back to where he had started.

CHAPTER FIFTEEN
BY JUAN

Fat Richie
El Gordo

[David] met Jonathan, the king's son. There was an
immediate bond between them, for Jonathan loved
David... And Jonathan made a solemn pact with David,
because he loved him as he loved himself.

1 Samuel 18: 1–3

WHEN I SAY I WAS always gone, always on the streets, and always out of the house, you could have bet that I was always with Richie, Fat Richie. He's been called Fat Richie as long as I can remember, because Tall Richie lived in the same neighborhood and ran with the same friends. Tall Richie, Fat Richie, and Ralph. Those were my boys. But Fat Richie and I, we became brothers.

Richie was born in Ciudad Juárez, Chihuahua, as I was. Unlike me, however, who started life with at least a few fluffy, decent, childhood memories, Richie's mother passed away before he turned two, after becoming pregnant and suffering complications with labor and delivery. His father reacted by sinking into such a deep depression that Richie's baby brother, whom his mother had opted to save while she was in labor, was given up for adoption to an aunt because his father was unable to cope with caring for him.

Juan and Richie

Many of Richie's earliest memories were waiting for his dad to pass out drunk on Friday nights so he could sneak his wallet and steal any money left from payday. Just a boy, Richie hid the money he lifted inside books throughout the house to ensure it would not all be spent on booze before the week was over. Initially, there was punishment for 'stealing' the money, but later in the week when they needed groceries or had to pay a bill, Richie would go to one of the hiding places and produce the necessary money. The sober version of his father would dole out hugs and tears and thanks that his son had taken care of things. This cycle went on for years.

Richie moved back and forth during these times, following the path of his father's alcoholism. He had very few friends because adults in town made fun of his dad, the drunk, and kids passed along the message, leaving Richie only two options: fighting to stick up for his father or saying nothing and being so sad and ashamed he couldn't look the kids in the face. He mostly chose to fight.

Sandra, Richie's much older sister, had resided in Texas for several years. When Richie was nine years old, she somehow got a visitor's

Visa and sent for him to spare him the fallout of his dad's drunkenness. Shortly after Richie's arrival in the States, he was in a terrible car accident that broke three of his vertebrae, so when he began a new school in a new country speaking no English at all, he also began in a neck brace.

Traumatized? Nope. Not Richie. He loved the attention it drew, and that it caused even more than normal interest in the 'new kid.' Everyone was kind to him, careful with him, and looked out for him. He was not used to having friends and not used to getting attention. This was such a new and different social experience than he'd had in the past, that he caught on and learned to speak English very quickly.

I met Richie when I was ten and lived at Fairway Crossing Apartments off of Ferguson in the heart of East Dallas projects. He actually met my big sister Nena, first. He had a crush on her, because everyone had a crush on Nena, and began to hang around outside our apartment with all of us. He moved back and forth from one family member to another because his dad got a different job, or whatever reason poverty or alcohol demanded that month. But we never lost touch. If Richie was living in town, we were together.

It didn't take much for us to bond deeply as brothers. The nonsense and trouble of typical teenage boys who had little or no supervision began to fill our days as we imitated troublemakers and gangsters around the neighborhood, like when we found a full carton of eggs on the side of the road. Not a dozen, but the double, 24 count cartons. The big ones. I mean, what would you have done? In my defense, I remember our actions started off innocently, seeing who could throw one the farthest. Then I guess that got boring because I'm pretty sure I ended up throwing the egg much farther than Richie... right into the side of a passing car!

Days were spent skipping school with a few friends, meeting at Whataburger, and planning to wander the streets all day. Skipping school worked until about 8:30 a.m. (we were not versed enough at skipping to make it longer than an hour without getting caught) when we cut across an alley and ran right into a friend's mom. Literally, we ran right into the side of her red car. We tried to run but weren't yet hardened enough in our criminal lives to be able to run without looking back. Plus we were scared of her! Except for Richie. He kept running.

Ma was furious with me, and her anger made me feel awful. Nena had gotten in a lot of trouble for skipping school, and I always thought "I'm not gonna be like that," yet there I was doing the same thing. I felt so guilty that I basically grounded myself for the next few days. But not Richie! He ran all the way back to school and made it back before first period was even over. He was marked present for every one of his classes.

Then there was the rock-throwing incident that ended with busted school windows and us being chased, and the stolen grocery cart we pushed as fast as we could down the hill in front of JFK Elementary until it crashed with one of us in it.

Neither of our families ever had money, so we often followed our hunger into Fiesta, the neighborhood grocery store, to snack on samples they were giving out. We also stole school supplies there because we never had any paper or pencils and we were bored and had nothing else to do. I guess we thought it was more humiliating to ask to borrow a pencil than to walk down the street looking ridiculous with packs of pencils and pens hanging out of our pockets.

We ran a lot from people yelling about our vandalism, and we hid a lot from people chasing us, but we only got caught a few times. All the while, the Lord was forging a bond between us to be one another's armor bearers.

At some point, in the midst of all of the running and hiding, the stealing and mischief, I invited Richie to Monday night Kids Club at YWAM with David Funke. I had begun to go pretty regularly on Monday nights because there were a lot of cute girls there. After the first time I invited Richie, he went any time I suggested it...for the food. The Lord speaks to us all in our own area of need, and Richie's area was always food!

Around that same time, people affiliated with Dallas Metro, another local church Alma was heavily involved in, came to the neighborhood and did programs every weekend. I knew Alma loved the church and the people, but she hadn't been able to lasso me in to going there. If I floated into anywhere, it was YWAM. However, one particular weekend close to Halloween when I was 14, the church brought a bus around and picked up all of the teenagers to go to an evangelistic program called Hell House. A cute girl I was interested in was on the bus, so I made Richie come along for the ride.

That was the night that my friend Richie asked the Lord to come into his heart! He heard about Jesus for the first time. He heard that God loved him unconditionally and sent His son to take away his sin and pain. He heard that no matter where he came from or who his family was or how abandoned he felt, God had chosen him.

At the end of the program, Richie wept for hours. There were tears for all the years of the roller coaster of his father's alcoholism, tears from the exhaustion of moving and running and being uprooted every few months due to poverty. Of being alone and motherless. Of struggle. Tears that shed layers of harsh walls Richie had put up to protect himself. God the Father comforted him and rooted things that had already been rooted inside of me, although they had not yet really begun to grow. Richie realized his whole life had been darkness and sadness up to that point. He was so tired of sadness. He knew he didn't want any more of it, and he learned there was another way.

I remember there was a change in Richie after that; a layer of hopelessness and weight was gone. There was a light in his eyes. I don't remember being happy for Richie that night, although I should have been. I just know I was happy because I sat by the cute girl the entire time!!

I had no idea that I was headed straight for the darkest, saddest moments of my life.

CHAPTER SIXTEEN

BY JUAN

Dad`s arrest
El arresto de Papa

A LL DURING MY time of wandering the streets of East Dallas with
Richie and the boys, Pa's drug use increased. It jumped from
alcohol and marijuana to crack and other things. I had no idea what he
was in to at the time; I didn't even know there were drugs. I just knew
he was an angry drunk who controlled our house with violent words
and fear. But Alma knew. She remembers Pa, *mis tíos*, even mom, once,
going into the restroom, sometimes alone, sometimes together, and
coming out sniffing and rubbing their noses. Alma even had a show-
down with Ma one time, confronting her, yelling, screaming, and begging her to look around and realize everything was falling apart, begging her to quit using, to quit partying. Sadly, Ma had been sucked in,
too. Where America had at first seemed to bring us better life, more
opportunity, all of a sudden, it seemed the money dried up. The drug
habits took it all; the need for drugs got so out of control, to the point
they sold things to keep it up. I would come home from school and my
game systems would be gone. One of Alma's most treasured posses-
sions, a gold necklace, mysteriously disappeared.

Juan's mother and Father, Juarez, Mexico, 2014

We didn't know then that it was addiction stealing them. Our family had known struggle before, and I guess we kids just thought it was another round of that cycle. We thought things would get better. Instead, the fighting and abuse became more intense. My cousin Gabriela—Gabby—and her boyfriend Cesar had just arrived in the United States. They had a daughter and wanted to give her a better life than they had experienced in México. They moved in with us at that time. The apartment was crowded, adding to the rising tensions, and none of us wanted to be there.

I had grown into a teenager, which in a Mexican family pretty much meant I was a man and had very little accountability. I took advantage of the freedom I had as the oldest, so I was almost always gone. *Nunca en casa.* Alma's escape was soccer, her friends, and her church. She was *always* at church. She was involved with Dallas Metro long before Richie or I ever went. I mentioned her tender heart earlier, tender to people and tender toward God. She was privy to many things inside our household that I missed: inner workings of my parents' relationship, the jealousy, control, innuendos about drugs, many things I never picked up on. It's amazing what she saw didn't harden her heart at a young age, but it didn't. She dragged those things to the Lord's feet and gave them all to Him.

She was an excellent soccer player; disciplined and dedicated. Sadly, no one ever went to Alma's soccer games or even paid the required fees for that matter. I realize now how much we were on our own even then, though we didn't yet know to look out for one another. She has since told me she remembers feeling humiliated and telling her coach on several occasions, "I can't play in this tournament, or this season, or buy this uniform, because we have no money. My parents can't come up with it." The coach knew she was dedicated and wanted her on the team and covered her expenses. Her friends' parents took her to games and cheered for her from the sidelines.

Luis and Isaac, my younger brothers, were still very small and hopefully unaware of the building tension and not in need of escape. They were always at home with Ma, unlike Alma and me. I have not yet asked them what they remember from that time. Maybe I am afraid to know. Maybe I feel bad that Alma and I were never home for them.

One day I did come home and everyone but Alma, Gabby, and Cesar was gone. *¿Dónde están?* "Where is everyone?" I asked.

Cesar said, "Your dad got arrested." My heart skipped a beat, but within a split second, Alma's mouth betrayed her, and one side of her lips curled up into a sly smile.

"Not funny," I growled, and they all began to laugh at the joke about dad getting arrested.

We had no clue how very *not* amusing it was, as dad's trouble with the law would soon be true.

When I came home a few months later, near Christmas time, Cesar was there and said those words again, as if rewinding the moment and pushing play. This time I mumbled, "Whatever," and kept moving. But this time, no one laughed. I saw no curves in the corners of anyone's mouth, and this time, Alma began to cry.

The night before, Ma had a funny feeling about Pa going out. She expressed her concern to him, but he shoved it off as just another way for his wife to nag and be upset about his absence, the drinking, and drugs. They fought, enough to wake us kids up in the night, and we got out of bed to see what was going on. *Va salir.* "He's going to leave," she said to us, her voice begging us to somehow to stop him. But what could we do? A friend came to get Pa, and they left. We all went back to bed. None of us really thought much of it, because it wasn't that uncommon.

The next morning we woke up to get ready for school, and Pa hadn't returned, which wasn't exactly normal, but it wasn't unheard of either, so I expected he would eventually trip in and be home later that night. But I returned home to a very different scenario. It was my cousin, Lalo, who knocked on the door to tell my mother that our father had been arrested.

Not long after that, I lost my family.

By this time, my oldest sister Nena had returned to México, for my grandfather was very ill. When we left Juárez, my *Abuelo* begged my mom to leave Nena with him. "I'll take care of her." He was basically the only father Nena had known, and she resented my father greatly through the years for dragging Ma into drugs, and for his abusive ways. Looking back, I know it really fell to her to take care of all of us while my parents were too strung out. For several years, when we were hungry, or needed something, we told Nena. So when *Abuelo* was sick and needed help, I'm sure she welcomed the chance to escape— the chance to return to Juarez.

The rest of us, though, were left struck by Pa's arrest. This whole process is blurry to me, as traumas usually are when we look back on them. Something that happens so fast and so slow all at the same time. You go back again and again to watch it on repeat in your head, to remember how it felt and smelled in the room when you found out your life had been altered in a split second. Very strange things stick out in your memory, while large chunks of time that should be there seem to be lost. You seem to be lost and floating around in an abyss.

That's how the next few days and weeks were with me. I do remember coming home the night he was arrested, when everyone had returned from spreading the news and looking into options about what to do next. We, of course, had no money for bail and weren't sure we were allowed to bail him out anyway, but when your family is ripped apart in an instant, it seems necessary to go, to scatter, to do something.

What I did was go to Kids Club. Up to that point, I had attended YWAM off and on, mostly for the social side of it. Tall Richie, Fat Richie, and Ralph went with me. They always fed us there, and it was fun; those were the reasons we went. But this evening, being there was different. One of the things racing through my mind, along with the fear and confusion, was a sermon I'd remembered hearing. I have no idea why it stuck with me when I heard it, or why it came to the surface in my mind that night, but it was all about not blaming God or being angry with Him when bad things happen, to lean into Him instead. I knew I needed to go to Kids Club. I needed God. When it was over, David Funke drove me home. I told him what had happened with Pa and asked if he would pray—I didn't know what else to do.

This moment began many years of throwing myself into the Lord and asking people I had a relationship with to carry me, to support me in prayer while I begged God to see me through. It was natural in those numb, shocked moments when there was nowhere else to go and I didn't know what to do except run to God. It would still be a while before I held onto Him all of the time, not just in my darkest hours.

Later that evening when I and everyone else returned home, we fell, one by one, into the bed on the floor. I don't remember exactly how it happened. Ma probably lay down beside Isaac to get him to go to sleep. Luis probably followed. One of them was no doubt crying out of confusion and from exhaustion at being hauled around all day, and Ma joined in, quiet tears falling out of utter loss at what to do next, which step to take, who to even talk to. Alma had stayed with a friend, and I, the big, macho Mexican teenage boy, stared out the window, determined not to cry. But looking down at the family bed of grief, I climbed in and was betrayed by a few quiet tears. Ma simply whispered in the darkness, *Tu también, mijo?* You, too, son? As if to tell me it was okay to cry.

We knew that Pa being arrested meant he was in danger of being deported. Communication with the courts and with the jail was sketchy. We did find out we could bail him out for $500, but seeing as we had begun moving every month or so because we had no money to pay bills and would be evicted, it may as well have been $5 million.

Because he was an illegal immigrant, Immigration was notified. It was then a countdown, a race to see who got to him first. If we bailed him out while still under City of Dallas jurisdiction, he would have had court fees, tickets, and small charges, but would not be deported, because Immigration is so overwhelmed they typically do not go hunting for a person. Had we been able to gather $500 and bail him out, who knows what would have happened differently. But given the path he was on, it may just have been a matter of time before he was picked up for something else. Or Pa's arrest could have been a wakeup call. Who knows?

What I know is that we didn't have the money and couldn't come up with the money. We tried to gather it from friends and family members and did come up with an amount that was close, but Immigration had already come to seize my father from the City of Dallas, and the opportunity for bail was gone. The air changed quickly. Clouds of hopelessness blew past the dirt and slithered over the Texas border as Juárez reached across to reclaim its grip on my father.

He was moved to a holding place for illegal immigrants and put on the path for deportation. It took forever to figure out where he was being held, but even then Ma was very afraid to go and visit because of the fear of deportation herself. Fear is a constant, uninvited guest that follows everywhere when you are an illegal, not sure what you are allowed to do and too afraid to draw attention to yourself to ask. A friend told my mom that she didn't need to worry about visiting; it wouldn't cause problems for her or for us kids, that they would let her in to see Pa with no hassle. No fear.

So we went, and we saw him through glass. In an orange jump suit. *Una vez*. One time. It was a building close to Lew Sterrett Jail, off of I-35 near downtown Dallas. I remember turning, in slow motion, past a McDonald's. I get chills to this day any time I pass that same McDonald's because I remember.

Alma didn't come with us. She had a soccer game. She was so deeply hurt and felt so abandoned and betrayed by our parents that she had no desire to miss out on one of the few positive things in her life, something that our family never supported her in, to go and visit Pa in the midst of the consequences of his own actions. She was probably right in her choice, although not coming and seeing Pa on that day is something that she has since wrestled with.

He was happy to see us. I remember because I thought the smile on his face a bit strange. I figured it was just relief to see us or pride in his family. My dad hadn't smiled much in a very long time.

The last time I had remembered him smiling was the best memory I had of him for many years. It's imprinted on my mind. I was walking through our tiny, cramped apartment. Dad was lying on the bed, no covers or anything, fully dressed, and it was cold. He had his arms crossed and wore a beanie cap on his head. As I walked past him toward the restroom, he lifted his head and looked at me. And smiled. He just smiled at me. His smile and his beanie. That was my last good memory of him.

I realize now his faint, fixed smile in the orange jumpsuit that day was a different kind of smile. It was much more about staying controlled and unemotional in that environment because in just minutes, he would have to return to being a prisoner. That smile was about trying to make us feel that everything was going to be all right, although he had a much greater understanding of what was about to happen than any of us did. He knew he was on his way back to México, and our family was about to be ripped apart.

He told me that day, through glass, in his orange jump suit, that I was grown now. It was my turn to be the man of the family and to take care of my mother, my sister, and my brothers, and he had that smile on his face when he said it. I had just barely turned 14. I was in ninth grade.

That's the very last time I ever saw my father.

He was deported shortly after that, right before Christmas.

CHAPTER SEVENTEEN
BY JUAN

Aftermath
La Consecuencia

THE FIRST FEW months after Pa was deported were so heavy. I remember having moments that seemed normal, like when I was outside hanging out with my friends, but then in an instant, I would remember and suddenly be gripped with sadness. The cloud. The whole atmosphere had changed. The apartment felt so hopeless all of the time.

Cesar, Gabby, and their daughter had moved out into an apartment above ours right before Pa was deported. We could no longer afford the apartment we were living in with no way to make rent and pay bills, so we had to move into an even smaller one than we'd been living in with Pa, next door to them. It was just one tiny bedroom and a small kitchen area for Ma, Alma, Luis, Isaac, and me, and a thick, thick cloud of sadness that took up a lot of space.

Ma had never worked before. I always thought Pa didn't want her to work, that he believed it was his job to provide and her job to take care of the kids. Alma has since corrected my thinking. She says Pa wouldn't let her out of the house. He was jealous and controlling and didn't want her to go 'out into the world'. The old school, Mexican *machismo*. He controlled her.

There she was, with all us kids, without Pa, and no work experience, no skills, no way to support her family. It was very scary. It was a bleak time that I don't remember many specifics about, just the heaviness in the air, the anticipation of the next thing to go wrong, the new crisis of the day.

During these months, she continued to receive news about my *abuelo* (grandfather), her father. He was sick, and his health was quickly deteriorating. It had always been hard for her to be away from her family. Leaving them behind had been the hardest thing about leaving México, especially at a time like this. But she was angry with Pa, disgusted with his addiction, and refused to follow him back to Juárez.

Family back home was torn. They wanted us to stay in America, to be educated, and to have a better life. We had already suffered the leaving and heartbreak of tearing away from our country, and they wanted us to reap the benefits, and have all of the hope the United States had to offer.

The realization of the "American way" is not something everyone here can achieve. Immigrants—illegal or not—come to this country for a better life. *La oportunidad*. That may seem strange to some Americans, since many of us continue to battle poverty or look over our shoulders wondering, waiting to be found out, or have a limitation put on us because we don't have papers or a social security number. Life is hard. But the truth is, hard life and lack of resources in America does not even come close to the devastating destitution in México. Low wages and hard backbreaking work are still work, and still wages, and that is something that is a hallucination back *en México*.

Though what we had in my childhood may not seem like much, and most would look and say I grew up poor, and even though we moved apartments every few months because we would get kicked out or couldn't pay, life was better and easier than in México. Ma's family wanted her—wanted us—to have that. They also wanted her to be able to see her father before he passed. They did not know which way to encourage her to go, and each family member she spoke to told her something different.

Abuelo told her she should return to be with my father. *Abuelo* was old México and worried what others might think; a wife should follow her husband. He was the only family member who felt that way, for my *tíos* (aunts and uncles) knew of Pa's abusive behavior, his drinking, and drug use and didn't want Ma running to follow him. They knew it was his poor choices that got him caught and charged. They wanted Ma and us kids to be free of him. They made it clear they would not support her decision to return home if it was to be with him.

It was an impossible choice; so many layers of emotion and fear and so many motivations. Which should she have looked to first? It was when *Tía Queta* (my aunt), told her of the severity of *Abuelo's* heart trouble and that if she wanted to see him alive, she should come home, Ma clearly made her decision.

CHAPTER EIGHTEEN
BY JUAN

The Road Back to Juárez
El Camino de Regreso a Juárez

THE FIRST TIME Ma brought returning to Mexico up to Alma and me, I thought it was a simple question, a family discussion. Like, *Let's take a vote.* "If we had the chance to go back and be with your dad and our family, would you want to go?"

I had no desire to return to Juárez. I was in school, I had friends, and, though to America we were illegals, we had grown out of México. America was what we knew and the only thing we remembered. We had heard our parents speak of the hardships in México our whole lives, that there was nothing but poverty, violence, dirt, and struggle there. There was no work, no opportunity. Everyone around us knew the situation in Mexico and told us how lucky we were to have parents who had gotten us out. We knew we didn't want to go back.

But later, we realized it was not a vote. Ma had decided to return, but given Alma's and my ages, she wanted to give us a choice. I think because she was so torn and unsure of the right path to take. So much of her, I believe, was afraid of returning to the vast nothingness of Juárez. Maybe she was even afraid of returning to Pa, but in her submissive Mexican wife way, she didn't know what else to do. I think part of her wanted to save us from what living in Juarez would be like.

She knew we considered ourselves to be American, and that's what she wanted us to be. She knew it was Pa's addiction and anger that had torn our family apart and that Alma and I should not be punished for it. She also knew she wasn't sure she was making the right choice. So for those reasons, and whatever else was hidden inside the heart of my mother, she allowed Alma and I to choose for ourselves.

At fourteen years of age, I had no idea all that choice would mean. I do know now it's not a decision any 14-year old should ever have to make.

So Alma and I chose to be American. We chose to be left in America.

Ma told Alma she was leaving and taking the younger boys with her. I guess I didn't believe her. I just couldn't imagine my reality without her, so I didn't know how to believe her, or wrap my brain around what it would look like to watch her go. The world as I knew it had been so recently rocked through the arrest and deportation of my father that I still lived in a daze.

Juan and his sister Alma, Dallas, TX, 2010.

So the night she left, I left too. I didn't stay to say goodbye to her—not really. I just said bye when I left, like I would have any other time, and went to church. I guess I didn't really think she'd be gone when I got home. But Alma stayed, and watched her drive away.

When I returned, she was gone, and so were my brothers. Being there without my Ma and Pa was strange, like floating outside my own body and trying to tell myself it was not real. But it didn't reach my guts that she was gone and it certainly didn't strike me that I couldn't see her or hug her ever again. I'm not sure it really has.

That was February of 2005, and I haven't seen her since.

Now, it may seem strange to you that she left us. I've been asked about her abandoning us many times—"How could she leave you? Weren't you mad at her?" But it angers me when people ask that because, in her mind, she was leaving us with family. We stayed with my cousin Gabby and her boyfriend Cesar when Ma left. She knew, or at least thought, we were taken care of. Her father was dying, and her husband was gone. What was she supposed to do? My mother didn't make a mistake; she made a decision.

Alma felt differently, feels differently today. She has more space inside of her to have several emotions at the same time, probably because women are more complicated and mysterious than men. I guess I only have room to assign it to one column in my brain and heart: good or bad. I know now that, had my mother made a different choice, had I made a different choice, I would be a much different person today. I am grateful for the road I've traveled and the person I've become, so I can only stamp my path as positive and file it under, 'Ma did the right thing.'

Alma went through a period of anger, feeling like Ma left because of Dad. She was exposed to conversations where family members told my mother things like, 'You know he's got someone else already. He's going to go on without you,' and, in turn, she saw Ma tormented with worry over my father's faithfulness. So in Alma's memories, Ma left us to return to Pa: his abuse, his anger, and his drug use. She's had times over the years of feeling like Ma chose Dad over her own children.

What a funny thing family is. Alma and I were the closest siblings in age, grew up the same way, and were both left here, in America, but we have such different takes on our lives. Such different reactions. I don't want to try and speak for Alma; I just want to tell my story. Yet Alma, her memories, and her reactions—different though they be— are part of my story—of what happened after we were left in America.

PART THREE
Crossing the Border
Cruzando la Frontera

"Without travel, I would have wound up a little, ignorant, white, Southern female, which was not my idea of a good life."
—*Lauren Hutton*

"Sin viaje, habría terminé una poquita mujer ignorante, blanca, del sur, y no era mi idea de una buena vida."
—*Lauren Hutton*

Border crossing El Paso, Texas into Juarez, Mexico

CHAPTER NINETEEN

BY SALLY

Descending into Dirt
Descender en Suciedad

A PLANE TO El Paso, reminding me of the one filling Juan's first view of free, American sky, a shuttle, and a taxi later, I stood at the foot of the Stanton Street Bridge in El Paso, Texas, looking in to México. The border guards, the same ones you see in movies carrying guns on their hips and sporting dark sunglasses, stopped and questioned me.

"What's the reason for your visit? Have you ever been to México before?"

I could see it. México. Juárez, the land that had created and birthed Juan, spit him out, and sent him on his way. I was looking at it; the country that had reclaimed his parents and thrown up an impenetrable wall between him and his parents. At the top of the arch of the bridge, two flags whipped in the wind. Huge flags. America, with its stars and stripes, and México with its red and green and its eagle. Right next to one another. Seeing both flags was surreal; so much so, that as I walked the incline of the bridge I reached for my camera to snap a picture of the line Juan could not cross. Within seconds,

Graffiti under the bridge at the border: "There are Dreams on This Side, too."

American border guards were at my side again. "Ma'am, you're not allowed to take pictures of the border. Not since 9/11." He saw the confusion on my face. "People could be scoping out how to cross. How to smuggle. How to..."

"Oh, that makes sense. I'm so sorry, I didn't know."

"We won't take your camera this time, but please delete the photo." The weight, the gravity of this line, this place where two countries meet, hit me in a new way. I have been to México a handful of times in my life, but never like this. Now, I was going to visit a family divided in two, on each side of this line. Never since 9/11, when rules are different, tighter security is necessary, and threats to America and its way of life are more real than ever. It was all more sobering than before.

I did not go to Juárez alone. My Spanish can normally get me by in most situations, but it is difficult to really express myself in another language, and I wanted to make sure I did not miss anything Juan

Sr. and Aurora had to say. Plus, my pasty skin and blue eyes needed a brown counterpart to have any chance of staying under the radar, so I was at ease with my translator by my side as we crested the top of the bridge and began descending the other side. The difference was immediate, and I felt overwhelmingly grateful to be American.

Beggars lined the bridge into Juárez, and hopelessness draped them like heavy winter clothes. Dirt. Dirt was everywhere. The street was so dirty it took my breath away, and I instantly wished I could take a shower. We walked far enough into the heart of the city where taxis would be a bit cheaper. As I bounced around the very bumpy back seat of that Mexican cab, I kept waiting to see the end of the dirt, waiting to see the part of the city that seemed finished and not dismantled as if it were under construction or had been ruined by something, but it never appeared.

A mere twenty five minutes after crossing the border, but a lifetime away from where I woke up in my hotel room that morning, we rounded a corner of, well, I can't even call it a street. It was as if someone had taken oversized matchboxes, thrown them from an airplane window to fall haphazardly to the ground, topped them with corrugated tin, and called it a roof. That's what the buildings looked like.

And there, in the middle of the road, stood Juan Sr. and Aurora Terrazas, waving their arms to welcome me.

CHAPTER TWENTY
BY SALLY

Puzzle Pieces
Piezas del Rompecabezas

AURORA, JUAN'S MOM, EMBRACED me with tears in her eyes. The first thing she said to me was, *Yo pensé que era mucho mas vieja.* "I thought you were much older!" I kind of laughed, not knowing exactly what to make of that comment, but soon realized it was because Juan and Alma had used the Spanish form of words that carried respect, the form you would use with an elder. They had given me a compliment. It meant they thought I was older and wiser. Yet there I stood in the dirt in jeans and tennis shoes with my hair in a ponytail!

I chuckled, imagining what this whole scene must have looked like to the neighbors. It seemed as though residents of Juárez, further in from the border like we were now, hardly ever used or saw taxis in their neighborhood. The view from where I stood looked like a third world country that hardly believed cars exist, even though we were only a few blocks from—what seemed to me—a pretty major street. So my taxi pulling in, blowing dirt behind it, made people turn and look. And what did they see when they turned? A white girl. A *very* white girl who looked like she didn't belong. I'm sure seeing me was as if an alien had landed to invade!

They ushered me into their building, through flies swarming around trash in the streets, and a curdled kind of urine funk that hung in the air. It was unbelievable to be there with Juan and Alma's parents, after having just been with them at my own house the night before. Juan Sr. escorted me in, pointing the way and inviting me to sit. The apartment, I guess it's called an apartment, was tidy. Concrete floor. Sparse. An old, beat up oven with utensils hanging above looking like they all got lots of use, and a small table made up the kitchen, which was actually just an open space that included the living room. There was a rough, steep staircase climbing straight up the wall, two very rugged, worn out looking couches, and an old bench seat that must have been taken out of the back of a van. Juan Sr. sat on the bench seat. The translator and I sat on the rugged couch lining one wall, and Aurora perched on the edge of the other couch, her knees touching mine. We gripped each other's hands almost the entire time I was there.

I had labored over a long list of questions. Juan and Alma had read them, highlighting any they thought might be touchy subjects. They had no idea how their father would react to being asked to talk about some of these things. They were almost as clueless as I was, having not been around him for many years. Also there was—well, this thing that seems to be common in Mexican families: no one asks questions. It's like an unwritten rule. Major life traumas or changes can happen—death, birth, break up, betrayal—and it is as if you are expected to walk into the room, notice the shift in the environment, whatever it may be, accept it, and move on. Don't talk about it. There were many things Juan and Alma had speculated about through the years, but were never sure of. One was drug use.

Juan was a little surprised one evening when he, Alma, and I had dinner, and Alma mentioned them using drugs. "They did?!" He had always assumed there was probably weed around and figured his dad had done drugs off and on, but he wasn't positive. He certainly never thought about his mom being involved with drugs. Alma had seen more and been aware of a lot more, but she still didn't know what kind of drugs, how long they had been using or to what extent either parent was involved. No one ever talked about the drugs and no one ever asked.

No one had even been able to tell me why Juan Sr. was actually arrested in the first place! They wondered if it was drug related, but never knew. One of them heard a relative talking about their dad hanging out with the wrong crowd, being innocent, and not realizing someone he was with was robbing a store. They didn't know if he was a victim or a criminal. Many pieces were missing from the puzzle, and filling those holes required some gut wrenching questions.

I had my list, but I'm not sure I used it; not even once. They both began to pour out their hearts like puddles on the floor in front of me. They took no prompting and seemed to have no hesitations. I instantly felt at ease, which was a strange emotion, considering the stories I was hearing: deep addiction that lead to severe neglect of family and children, crimes committed in pursuit of the next fix, Nena, the oldest daughter, being the caregiver because the parents were too strung out. These stories seemed like they could not possibly belong to the two people sitting in front of me now, the two that had waited in the road and waved their arms in the air at the sight of my taxi.

Juan Sr. told me that, as he disappeared more and more intensely into darkness, addiction and rage, it became a common practice for him and a few guys he ran with to rob for their drugs. He said their favorite picks were 7-11 stores and Payless Shoes. He kept using the Spanish verb that translates as 'rob' which painted a picture in my head of holding people at gun point and having them empty the cash registers. As he continued talking, though, I realized they would steal shoes from Payless to sell, or cigarettes, beer, and food from corner stores, both for their own use as well as extras to sell for the next hit.

It was during one of these ventures that Juan Sr. was waiting in the car, when his buddies inside stealing were caught. The police quickly identified Juan Sr. and the car he was driving as suspicious and asked the two criminals they'd just apprehended if this guy was with them. They both denied being with him and Juan Sr. thought they were going to let him go, until they searched his car. He was arrested because they found a crack pipe and other drug paraphernalia littering the back seat.

As soon as he finished that part of his story, and as soon as I had a huge puzzle piece fit into a hole that had been left in the entire picture, I sank back into the old couch. It seemed strange to know things about Juan and Alma, about their family, about their history; things that led to them being orphaned, being left in America. It felt wrong to know things about parents that their own children did not yet know. I had answers to questions that Juan and Alma had never asked. And I was going to have to go home and tell them.

Back Row: Nena's son Caleb, Sally, Nena (Juan's older sister), Aurora & Juan Sr. (Juan's mother and father). Front Row: Nena's daughter Lupe, a neighbor, & Isaac (Juan's youngest brother), in Juarez Mexico, 2014

PART FOUR
Left In America
Dejado en América

"I dreamed of you every night. It felt so real. And when I'd wake up the next morning, it was like your disappearance was fresh. Like you'd left me all over again."
—*Brodi Ashton, Everneath*

"Sueño de ti cada noche. Se sintió tan real. Y cuando me despertaría la próxima mañana, fue como tu desaparición era de nuevo. Como si me has dejado de nuevo."
—*Brodi Ashton, Everneath*

CHAPTER TWENTY-ONE

BY JUAN

A Few Wake up Calls
Unas Llamadas de Despierto

S O THERE WE were, Alma and me. Left behind. It was as if the rest of the family had been getting smaller and smaller on the horizon as they got farther and farther away. Then they disappeared. As surreal as it all was, it began to smack me in the face that I was on my own and that it would be up to me to make something of my life, as much as that can possibly sink in with a 14-year-old. Being on my own became a wakeup call. Without it, I would have become a very different man.

I had been running the streets with Fat Richie, Tall Richie, and Ralph long before my parents left. They never really disciplined us kids—I don't think they knew how—so I had really been making my own choices for a while. When I looked around, the 'norm' was not to care, not to worry about what you would become or what the future held. This is what happens with poverty mentality, no one expects anything good. Even when horrible things happen, like your father being deported, life just goes on; nothing is more serious or more important than anything else. The only thing that is valued is the moment, so why should I take school or anything else seriously? So far, I had been spared getting into any real trouble, but I was living dangerously close to that line. Close to being hardened.

I had a lot of anger, and it wasn't just because Ma and Pa had left. I guess it came from being poor, tiptoeing around Dad's rage, and the heaviness that had returned to the family. I had already started down a road of temper and aggression, especially with Alma.

There came an instant when I knew I had to change. I remember it crystal clear. There had been some teenage drama concerning a girl that caused a little tension between Richie and me, and Alma was asking me about it. *Was I mad at Richie? What was going on?* Her questions annoyed me because I didn't really have an answer for her, and it infuriated me that she was bringing it all up. Why was she in my business? My cousin Gabby was there and tried to mediate. "She cares about you, *Toño*. She knows you and Richie have always been tight, and she doesn't want to see you fighting."

"Yeah," Alma echoed.

I reached up and smacked her in the face. "Shut up. Stay out of my business," I hissed. Alma put her hand to her cheek and looked at me, only a bit shocked into silence because it wasn't totally unheard of for me to treat her this way. But Gabby didn't stay silent.

"Oh, so you want to be just like your dad? You want to treat Alma like he treated your mom?"

Suddenly, I was the shocked one because she was right. I was spitting hateful words at Alma, and she hadn't done anything to deserve them. I had taken the peace in the room and ripped through it with rage. I had put my hands on Alma to hurt her. I was bigger, meaner, and stronger, and I used my strength to shut her up. All of a sudden I realized it was all so familiar. The looks on Alma's and Gabby's faces were like a punch in the stomach. I used to have the same look. I had become the very thing I hated about my father; I had just done what he did to us for years. He had controlled us with a fear that so affected the family that we held each other at arm's length and all walked on eggshells. I had hated it, the feeling of fear.

I knew I had to be different. I knew I needed to stand guard of my heart, channel my anger, and not lash out. My dad had told me I was the man of the house and asked me to take care of the family, a family that had been ripped apart by the patterns he put into place. I knew I couldn't take care of myself, let alone the family, by following those same patterns.

It has been God's absolute grace on my life, and I can't even tell you how it happened, but that anger melted. It has been something I have not had to wrestle with too badly ever since that day when God showed me my own heart.

It was a moment that changed me.

In the months after Ma's return to México, that change helped me realize my family was depending on me. Not only was it up to me to make something of myself, to walk a different path than my parents or risk ending up just like them, but also I knew Ma and Pa were returning to poverty, that Alma was here with me, and that I wanted to have a life that would put me in a position to help. I knew that my dream would never happen if things continued the way they were.

So I started paying more attention in school. I started trying.

No one really knew what was going on or that my parents were gone, besides Richie, who at that time went to a different school than me. Years later, I went with a few friends to visit an English teacher I had in ninth grade. Reminiscing, she turned to someone to explain, "In the beginning of the year when Juan was in my class, he played around, he didn't care, and he never tried. But for some reason, all of a sudden, in the middle of the year, he changed. He turned in to a wonderful student."

To this day, she doesn't know what caused the change, but hearing her say that I had changed made me realize that I had been dead set on being a different kind of man than my father.

The Lord altered my path that year, although I wasn't aware of it. I thought I had overcome my anger and become dedicated to school in my own strength. I look back now, though, knowing that if those two wakeup calls had not happened so soon after my parents left, I would be a very different person today.

CHAPTER TWENTY-TWO
BY JUAN

Cesar

GABBY, MY COUSIN in her early twenties, had told my mother she would look after Alma and me. Her boyfriend, Cesar, was not much older, but declared himself the man of the house where Alma and I now lived.

Alma didn't last very long living there, for she and Gabby bumped heads a lot over house cleaning and how things should be done and taken care of. Alma had become good friends with a pretty solid family unit at the time, so it didn't take her long to leave. She moved in with her friend Sylvia and lived there for quite some time. Sylvia's mom had been a good friend of our family for many years, even godmother to both of my little brothers, so she was like family—*la comadre*.

Alma, in her young wisdom, was able to leave without a big blow up before things got bad between her and Gabby. I was not afforded that chance. I suppose in a measure of young testosterone, Cesar and I began to have confrontations about things. He was always on my back about something: my shoes were in the wrong place, or why hadn't I done this? What was I doing now? He didn't seem that much older than me, but I suppose since he was the only one around to rebel against, that's where I aimed all of my teenage angst.

Or maybe he was just that unreasonable.

Who knows? In my mind, he was unreasonable, but I was a 14 year old kid!

When I got home from school one Monday night and was getting ready to go to church at YWAM's Monday night service, there was a new series of frustrations. My shoes were under the black rocking chair. 'They don't go there.' 'Take out the trash.' 'What are you doing?' 'Pick that up!'

By the time my dad had been arrested, I wasn't even really taking orders from him anymore; we had an unspoken understanding since Ma had talked to him about hitting me. So I certainly didn't feel like being bossed around by Cesar. I was fed up. I left for church knowing I needed a break from that house for a little while. I walked down the stairs from our second story apartment and looked back over my shoulder. Cesar was there, glaring out the window, watching me leave. I felt the hatred seething, even from out the door and down the stairs.

I asked Ralph if I could crash with him for a few days. I went to school during the day and would swing by the apartment afterwards for clothes and food. I went by when I knew Cesar and Gabby were at work because I didn't want to show up at Ralph's hungry every night, for they were already doing me a favor letting me stay there. I figured, give it a few days, then go home to talk with Gabby, and clear a few things up when Cesar was not home.

It didn't exactly work that way.

I went Sunday night because I knew Cesar worked late Sundays, and Gabby would be home about 10:00. I got to the apartment around 8:00, hung out a while, and called Alma. She had heard I'd been gone all week, but we hadn't spoken and I figured she would worry, so I called to fill her in. She knew how cranky Cesar could be and let me vent. When I heard the door open, I told Alma I'd call her later after I spoke with Gabby and let her know how our conversation went. I hung up, and walked into the living room where... I came face to face with Cesar and his friend.

¿Que haces aquí? "What are you doing here?" He slurred, and I immediately knew he had been drinking. Gabby was nowhere around. It had been Cesar coming home, not her!

"I just want to talk to Gabby," I said.

"Well, I just want you to get out! I don't want you in my house." *¡Sácate!*

I looked straight into Cesar's eyes; he was part of the tiny shred of family I had left. "Why do you want me out so bad? What have I done to you?" I pleaded.

Nada. No mas que no te quiero. "Nothing. I just don't like you."

I winced. I knew Cesar got on my nerves, but I was devastated over losing my parents. I didn't hate Cesar; I just didn't like being bossed around and nitpicked when I felt like I was really trying at school and wasn't a bad kid. His words pierced me. He was one of the only people left in my life, and he spit hateful words at me.

He stared me down and his friend stood up. My face stung. I was freaked out and unsure of how drunk he was or what he would do if I didn't leave, so I dropped my apartment key at his feet. "There."

'Dámelo,' he barked. "No. You pick it up."

"You better get out of here before I call the cops," he hissed.

I was shaking with rage, fear, and confusion. What just happened? As I walked out the door and down the stairs away from the building, Cesar yelled into the darkness, "Get back here!" Hadn't he just kicked me out? And now he was following me and bellowing drunken words— to this day I don't know if they were more threats, or regrets, or what.

I was humiliated and scared; there was no way I was going back. There was also no way I wanted him catching up to me, so I yelled over my shoulder to Cesar's friend, "You better get your boy away from me!" Spewing curses back at him, I kept walking until I got to the end of the street and ducked into the alley. I froze. I stood there with my heart pounding. Aching. I had been walking fast, but toward where? There was nowhere to go. The only thing I knew to do was pray.

"God, what am I supposed to do? My parents are gone. I'm only fifteen. I have nothing and nowhere to go," I cried.

The word homeless didn't occur to me then. Nor did it ever in the next several years, I don't think, but it must have occurred to Ralph's mom because that was the only place I could think of to go—back to Ralph's. I told him what had happened and then crashed into a hopeless sleep. When I woke up, they had brought me an ice cream cone.

Juan's cousin Gabby, Gabby's daughter Fany, and Juan's sister Alma, January 2015.

CHAPTER TWENTY-THREE
BY JUAN

The Widow and the Orphan
La Viuda y El Huérfano

THE NEXT FEW years are difficult to tell in any sort of order or importance. It was a time of blurry bouncing from one thing to the next. Total defense, reacting to forces outside my control. Autopilot. Survival mode. Only a few things stick out as significant or worthy of telling because most of my life felt like it was being dragged along by a current, my feet not finding sturdy ground beneath me as I tried to keep my head up. I felt numb, as if I were in a daze. I had no idea what I was doing or what I would become, and many, many times, I thought I would not survive.

I stayed at Ralph's for a while, probably about a month. His mother was kind to me, and in the years that followed, you could say she was the nearest thing I had to a maternal figure. Not nurturing or caring necessarily, just aware enough to notice if I had eaten anything or not and bossy enough to make me if I hadn't. She was one of the few who never acted bothered or put out to have me around. She was the closest thing to a mom I have had since México reclaimed mine.

Juan and Ralph's mom Carla, dancing.

She was cool, more like a friend to us than a mother. She let her house be a hub, and lots of teenagers spun in and out of its headquarters. She was really a very special woman.

I could have stayed longer than a month—I knew that. She did not kick me out, Ralph and I didn't have a fight... I was just aware that they were already broke, and I was a burden. I was another mouth to feed. This became a pattern of thought for me, no matter who I was with. 'Don't be a burden. Don't wear out your welcome.'

So I kept moving.

Richie had been staying at the Dream Center, an extension of Dallas Metro, in some housing they had for young adults who were being discipled or making major changes in their lives. Richie wasn't exactly a young adult, but an older guy named Vincent was living there in the program and didn't mind Richie crashing with him. The housing wasn't meant for kids. Richie was still a minor and should not have been allowed to stay, but he needed a structured place to stay and go to school, it just couldn't be 'official.' Everyone kind of pretended he didn't really live there so it wouldn't be breaking the rules. They cared about him and looked after him.

Juan, Richie, and James Musyoki at Dallas Metro Summer Camp, 2006

They gave him a home.

I knew he liked it there, and with the feeling that it was time for me to leave Ralph's creeping up, Richie and I decided I should stay with him. Ha! We decided. We had absolutely no control over anything that was happening in our lives. We had no authority or permission to decide I should move in with Richie to a place *he* wasn't even supposed to be staying! I suppose discussing it made us feel like we had options.

So I moved in, which just meant I started sleeping there.

Vincent, Carl, James—other young men who lived at the Dream Center and walked with the Lord—began inviting us to hang out, play ball, and go to Bible Studies. They included us in everything they did. We spent tons of time with them. We loved that time and didn't even realize we were being ministered to. We were just glad to have something to do, and we felt cool to be included with older guys.

For me, living at the Dream Center was a season of gathering information through Bible study and being exposed to scripture. I even attended an intense discipleship training school with these guys. The school was more than a roof and some mad wrestling matches; I was

Vincent Morelos of Dallas Metro, one of the few times it snowed in Dallas.

Carl and Cerrissa Trevino of Dallas Metro with their daughter Carli Trevino.

learning things about submitting to authority, how to walk in humility, and about the fruits of the spirit. These young men took me in and spent their lives with me. I still wasn't broken before the Lord, but that would come. This period of time deepened my knowledge of the Bible and developed character in me. I was even baptized on July 26, 2005, at Dallas Metro. God began a good work in me there. I didn't just dive in or understand all of it fully.

I still felt guilty for being sneaky. Pastor Clay was the Pastor at Dallas Metro, and I had great respect for him. I didn't like having to be dishonest with him and pretend I wasn't staying there. He was the boss, and I knew it was against the rules for me to stay, but I always felt like he knew. I figured he must not have had the heart to kick us out, so he just pretended not to notice we were around so much, and he never asked questions. I think on purpose.

We were orphans, I guess. That's probably how people saw us. Even as I write my story now, it feels strange. Like the Bible says in James 1:27, *"True religion is this: to care for the widow and the orphan..."* I never saw myself in that verse, but I guess people like Ralph's mom, Vincent, the other guys, and Pastor Clay did. They knew I was on my own, an orphan, so they cared for me.

CHAPTER TWENTY-FOUR
BY JUAN

Almost Family
Familia... Casi...

WHILE STAYING AT the Dream Center, I was around Dallas Metro a lot and ended up attending summer camp with their youth group after my sophomore year of high school. When I returned, I heard from Alma that my brother Luis had come back to Dallas from Juarez for the summer. Mom and Dad had been gone about a year at this point, and Alma still lived with *la comadre,* the family friends.

Remember, Luis was born a U.S. citizen and had the privilege of deciding on which side of the border he wished to reside. He missed Alma and me, and Ma still wanted better opportunities for him. *La comadre* had agreed to allow Luis to stay for a while and see how it went. Ma gave the friends Luis' social security number so they could claim him on their taxes and get the dependent benefit as a sort of payment for looking after him.

I saw this as an opportunity to reunite and be somewhat of a family. The Dream Center was far across town, especially for kids with no license, car, or bus fare. Staying there had made it hard ever to see Alma and now Luis. I knew I couldn't move in with *la comadre;* having all 3 of us there would be too much of a strain, but my *Tía Licha* (aunt) lived near there, and I thought being close was a good option. I asked her if I could stay with them for a while, explaining that I wanted to be near Alma and Luis. She told me I would need to speak with my uncle. I nervously approached him; he said yes, but I knew it was a strained yes, something he wasn't thrilled about. I heard it in his voice. They didn't have a lot of money and were supporting kids of their own, so I vowed not to be a burden. I really just needed a place to sleep.

It worked for me, but I was still going to school far away and playing football. I would come home late at night after practice, and Luis would be upset that I wasn't around more. He wanted to stick to me like glue, so he spent a lot of time sitting and waiting on me to get home.

I think it was a season of loneliness for Luis, of feeling abandoned and forgotten, so I wasn't surprised when he went with *la comadre* back to México for a visit and decided to stay. The idea of holding our family together sounded good to me, like I was being the man of the house my father had asked me to be, but I was still a kid. I didn't know the strength it took to grip a family that was tearing at the seams.

Luis had been the reason I had moved back to that side of town, the only reason I had asked *Tía Licha* if I could stay, and after he returned to México, things felt a bit strained. I still played football, had late practices, games, and so forth, but I also didn't have Luis to come home to, so I stayed gone even more. When I came home late my uncle would fuss at me. "I don't understand why you have to be gone so much." I was used to feeling like a burden in the places I had been staying, but now it was upsetting if I was gone too much?

After a year of house hopping and never quite feeling like I belonged anywhere, it was strange to be with family, to begin to feel like they were responsible for me and cared what I did, and like I needed to be responsible and care what they did. To be home on time or to be part of the way the household ran was foreign to me. I was close to my cousins, always had a great time with them, and I began to feel comfortable thinking of this as a place I lived and not just a place I was staying. It was kind of like a home to me.

There's even a lesson my uncle taught me that I try and hold on to today. He was getting on to me about helping around the house. Not harshly, just normal teenage stuff. He took me to the front yard and pointed around.

'See these leaves everywhere? All over the sidewalk, the yard, the porch all the way up to the house? I've been watching them. They're not going anywhere. I want you to take care of them.' So I did. He thanked me the next day, adding, 'You know, *Toño*, you don't have to wait to be asked to do something. You can look around, see what needs to be done and do it. That's the way it should be.'

It seems simple, now, the way a family unit operates, but then I hadn't had a family unit in a while and never really actually had a functioning one. It was a good lesson. I realized he could 'boss' me without anger, something I had never experienced with my own parents. I realized I should be more aware and notice things. I wanted to be helpful. I started to feel at home there… for a while.

I loved cereal. I ate it all the time at Licha's house. Before school, after practice, late at night, I ate it all the time. In fact, it's about the ONLY thing I ate at Licha's house, so when there started to be no milk in the fridge, I definitely noticed. For a few days I thought, 'No biggie. Someone will go to the store.' After a week, I thought having no milk was weird. I never would have asked. I was more comfortable living there than I had been anywhere else, but I was still far from saying things like, 'Hey, where's the milk?'

Then one day I was hanging out with my cousins. They were like siblings to me, which felt great being far from my brothers and sisters. They had a miniature fridge in their room, and my youngest cousin went to get something out of it. And I saw it. A gallon of milk, hidden away from me.

It seem like a small thing, but it pierced me. They were hiding the milk from me! I was a burden. I was mad at myself for letting my guard down and thinking that my time of house hopping was over, for thinking that I actually belonged and didn't have to worry about spending too much time there or eating their food. I had begun to feel living here was different, but this was a slap in the face that made me realize that I was the same here, as everywhere else. I was an imposition. I was almost family, related, but not part of their immediate circle, and the hidden milk was a huge, flashing sign reminding me that I didn't belong there.

I was so hurt and felt so shunned. I packed my few things and told them a friend had offered for me to stay with them, and that it was closer to the school or something. I don't really remember what I told them. I just remember it was almost December of 2006. I had stayed with them a few months through the fall. To this day, I have never told them the real reason that I left.

CHAPTER TWENTY-FIVE
BY JUAN

A Little too Familiar
Un Poco Familiar

CRASHED BACK AT Ralph's for a while. They always took care of me, but honestly I didn't love staying there because their home was a reminder of the strain of my own childhood with my own family. They had almost nothing and struggled to put food on the table as well. Many times, I preferred not to eat rather than take food from them, but that's when the maternal side of Ralph's mama would kick in. "Boy, you better get over here and eat something 'fore I...."

Part of the reason I would have preferred not to eat many times was that his mom always made beans. I hated beans. They smelled like poverty to me; they still do. Without even really being aware of it, something inside of me had resolved to distance myself from what I thought at the time were any stereotypical Mexican behaviors: eating nothing but rice and beans, being poor, even speaking Spanish. Some of my thoughts were conscious, and some weren't, but I knew I was an illegal immigrant. I knew there was always a danger of being "sent back", so to me, there was danger in appearing to be anything like a poor Mexican, a 'wetback.' I had become painfully aware that I was born in México, and wasn't from America; that I wasn't *supposed* to be here. Being reminded of what it would be like to be sent back, though, made me realize just how Americanized I was. I couldn't imagine leaving my home in the U.S and moving back to Mexico. Because even though I really had no home, I was American.

Therefore, being connected to any Mexican stereotype made me crazy. I began to feel that the typical Mexican was weak: the drama of *novelas*, needing someone to translate for you, to rescue you, and struggling to survive. To me, typical Mexicans had no voice, and I wanted to be heard.

Everywhere I looked, the people who seemed to get attention in the American culture were the athletes or the rappers. To me the African American culture represented strength in every way I perceived Mexicans to be weak at the time. I began working on my language, my accent. I still spoke Spanish some, but only when I had to. I carried a dictionary with me and wrote down any new words I heard. I wanted to improve my vocabulary, to come across as smart and strong. I wore baggy clothes, hung out with athletes, hung out with strength.

My coloring is pretty dark, not the typical Mexican caramel, but a deeper, darker tint under the skin, and my hair, well, my hair served me well in those days! It's almost like an afro, so lots of people assumed I was half Black, and I didn't dispute it.

I guess associating with Black culture felt safer to me. They weren't in danger of being told to go back to where they came from or of anyone saying they didn't belong. My feelings about my culture, my people, are things the Lord has done much work on in recent years. It took stripping layers of anger from my parents' choices, from growing up poor, and from having to prove that I belong here. It took some maturing and perspective before I could be proud of my heritage again.

But back then, staying at Ralph's and smelling beans, watching the labor it took to survive; it was all just a little too familiar.

CHAPTER TWENTY-SIX
BY JUAN

Manna from Heaven[6]
Manna del Cielo

HOUSE HOPPING BECAME my specialty. Ralph's, the Dream Center with Richie, and the couches of friends from school after football practice. Don't stay anywhere too long. Don't be a burden.

I continued to attend North Dallas High School, though. I resolved early on when I found myself on my own that I would stay and finish school, going all four years at North Dallas. We moved around so much in my early elementary years that it felt like an accomplishment to stay rooted to something. And I didn't want to leave my friends. I look back now and realize it truly was a miracle that the Lord saw me through and kept me there, but back then it just felt like a simple choice I made.

---

6 Psalm 78:23–25 *"When the children of Israel were stuck in the wilderness, God provided manna from Heaven for them to eat. They did not have to strive to find food. He provided it for them, even in the midst of the years they were cast out."*

It wasn't simple; there were many complications. One was that I was called into the office at school several times and asked about my residency. They needed to know that North Dallas was actually my home school. 'We sent this letter to your parents and it was sent back.' I would say we had just moved, and I didn't know my address. Then they would ask for a bill. I'd tell them to give me a few days and I'd get it to them. That would last a while, and I avoided the office like the plague. Miraculously, they never followed through to realize that, not only did I live out of district for North Dallas to be my home school, but I actually lived nowhere and had no supervision. It was like God put blinders on their eyes and hid me from their view.

Another difficulty was that some of the places I stayed were far from school, like when I stayed at the Dream Center. I would leave to catch the city bus as early as six each morning to get across town in time. The challenging part was that I had no income, no assistance, no job, no money. And it costs money to ride the bus. Miraculously, each and every single day, for years, I had a dollar for the bus. Sometimes I would find change, or sometimes someone who knew my situation would hand me one. Whatever it was, it was God's provision to me.

In my junior year of high school, another gift was introduced to me, though I didn't unwrap it until much later. I realized that David Funke went to church. It makes me laugh at myself now that I never thought about it before, but I guess I thought YWAM and Kid's Club *were* David's church, and that he was the pastor. By this time, Richie had adopted YWAM as his family, and they had invited him in as theirs. At YWAM one day, Richie actually invited me to go to church with them. We climbed into the van and went to youth group at Trinity Dallas, the church David attended. It was such a different universe!

The only church I knew other than YWAM was Dallas Metro, which was filled with people like me, even worse than me, in my mind: messed up, broken, coming off the streets, hard core lives. No one there grew up in church or had known scripture before, but at Trinity, the youth leader, Dustin Sample, who was new at the time, would say from the front of the room, "Turn to such and such and find verse *blah, blah, blah,"* and the room filled with the sound of flipping pages. I mean, these kids knew where Habakkuk was! Richie, Ralph, and I were stunned. We knew we were way out of our league!

At Dallas Metro, they talked about Jesus, but here, they were studying the Word! It was such a different place, a different group of people. To me, they appeared to have it all together. They knew scripture, had families, and had money. I figured they must not struggle with anything. The guys and I were outgrowing Kids Club, but had continued to weave in and out of YWAM and Metro at different times. But beginning my junior year, when I floated into YWAM, it meant floating into Trinity Youth Group, under the leadership of Dustin, with all of these white kids who had it all together.

The thing was, that as I spent time with them here and there over months, I got to know them and saw something I never had before. Apparently, white kids struggled, too. Apparently, having a family and having money didn't mean you had no problems. I had always assumed that if I had a home, if my family were together, and if money didn't always escape me, life would be easy. But I got to know these kids who seemed so different than me. I got to know their hearts and their lives. I saw that they knew the Lord and loved the Lord, but they were broken, too, like me. I can't explain it, but I needed to see that, and God showed it to me.

That was just the beginning of many things He would show me through watching the youth group at Trinity, through watching the youth leader, Dustin, through watching other men and families I met there. Like Scott Robson. He seemed to walk and talk as a godly man and father, like no one else I'd ever seen, and soon he would walk beside me. There was the Strickfaden family, who seemed to love *everyone* and took many into the shelter of their wings, eventually taking me in as one of their own. Through these godly people, I slowly began to see that knowing God and loving God meant more than knowing the Bible or having things go your way. For the first time, I began to watch a spiritual family. As I became involved little by little at Trinity, that's mostly what I did for a long time. I watched as if I were daring the Lord to make Himself real to me, daring Him to show me how life could possibly be better and how I could have peace and a family. He began to.

God was giving me little gifts all of the time those days. Out of teenage self-centeredness and immaturity, I just couldn't recognize how much He was tending to me. I didn't know He was, *"hiding me in the shadow of His wings,"*[7] blinding the eyes of the secretary and principal at North Dallas to my residency, miraculously plopping a dollar into my hand for the bus every day, showing me kids who were so different than me, yet still struggled, and painting pictures in front of me of what family could look like. This was Him taking care of my needs, even though I didn't know what they were. I never sought out these gifts. They just happened. Appeared. Like manna from Heaven.

---

7   Psalm 57:1 *"Have mercy on me, my God, have mercy on me, for in you I take refuge. I will take refuge in the shadow of your wings until the disaster has passed."*

CHAPTER TWENTY-SEVEN

BY JUAN

A Rough Roof
Un Techo Duro

F OR QUITE SOME time, most mornings I was at the Dream Center. I would have found my dollar somewhere and be getting ready for school. Let's just say Richie didn't always go to school, so I would be up and around that early by myself. Just me. Well, just me... and Pastor Clay.

Like I said, Pastor Clay knew Richie and I were around, but he didn't KNOW Richie and I were around because we weren't supposed to be staying there. He didn't ask, and we didn't tell. The problem was in the mornings when I left to catch the bus for the long ride to school, Pastor Clay was up walking the property, praying, and spending time with God before the sun came up. I didn't want him to officially know I was staying there, so I used to have to sneak by the praying man!

One morning though, I came outside, headed down the stairs toward the bus stop, and came face to face with him. We made eye contact, and he said in a flat sort of voice I couldn't really read, "You on your way to school?"

Pastor Clay Wallace and his wife Barbara of Dallas Metro at Juan's graduation from El Centro College in 2011.

Yes sir," I answered. He just nodded. Later that week, he sat me down. I wondered if he was angry. I braced myself, like I would have done in my childhood when I didn't know what mood my father was in. "You know you and Richie aren't supposed to be here, right? I mean, if something happened to you, or you got hurt on the property, I could get in a lot of trouble." The Dream Center, Dallas Metro, and I could be sued. I would be liable."

I was waiting for him to tell me I couldn't be there, that he didn't want me staying there anymore, but he didn't. "I know your situation," he said, "and I want to do what I can. You understand?" I nodded. I was still waiting; surely he was angry, but his anger never came. He didn't yell or exercise his power; instead, he granted peace and grace. He just wanted me to understand.

That was the last time he ever brought up my living situation. He 'pretended' not to see us or know we were there. He never ran us off. Not once. I believe he sat me down for that talk to let me know he trusted me. He dealt with me in such a different manner than almost any adult ever had, and the way he treated me stayed with me. He couldn't officially give me permission to live under that roof, but he was letting me know he wasn't going to take the roof away. From that moment on, as I floated in and out of the Dream Center, I took it to heart that Pastor Clay was putting himself on the line for me. I wouldn't stay too long at one time, and when I did I was really careful to stay out of situations where I could be hurt or injured or anything that would draw attention to the fact that I was there.

Richie stayed there steadily, but I drifted in and out. The way the Dream Center apartments worked was that people or families in need would move in for a time, get on their feet, receive ministry, be discipled, and then move out. The rest were home to church staff. Richie bunked with different guys he was friends with at first, but after a while, there wasn't anyone left he knew well. Someone was, however, always moving out, so he crashed in whatever apartment was empty at the time. The bad part about that plan was it meant the utilities in empty apartments wouldn't always be on. Richie was pretty handy, though, and would rig at least one electricity outlet from an apartment below us, or next to us, to an extension cord fed through a window so we could use it.

Water and gas for the stove were another story. We had hardly any food, of course, but we could always come up with Ramen Noodles. Cooking Ramen with no electricity is tricky, though. We put it in a bowl, poured a little hot water over it, and just let it sit. If it sat long enough, it would get soggy, as if it had been cooked. Sort of.

One time a girl we each had a crush on—her mom knew our situation—gave us a package of tortillas. We feasted on those! I remember eating tortillas for days and feeling so lucky! I look back now on those times and laugh; laugh at how goofy we were, laugh at some of the things we did, and laugh at how we survived. It seems rough to think about our struggles, but they were a gift. Pastor Clay never ran us off and kept a roof over our heads, no matter how rough the Ramen noodles or the roof was!

CHAPTER TWENTY-EIGHT

BY JUAN

Running Out of Options
Agotando las Opciones

B Y THE END of my junior year I felt like a ping-pong ball. Not wanting to stay at the Dream Center for too long of a stretch after my talk with Pastor Clay, I was always looking for options. I had some friends who got their own apartment, and I crashed with them a while. Living there was easier, closer to school. It wasn't a good situation, though. They used the apartment like most high school kids on their own would have, as a place to chill, to drink, and to get high. Miraculously, alcohol and drugs were never temptations for me. I don't know if it was because I had seen what alcohol and drugs did to my dad, but I always felt something telling me not to go down that road, that I was different. It has truly been the hand of God that has spared me from that snare.

As far as getting in trouble, though, I knew it didn't matter if I were doing the drugs or not. If anything ever happened, and my friends got busted, I was at an apartment with high school kids and drugs. No one would believe I wasn't involved; I would automatically be included because I was there. I knew I couldn't stay there any longer.

A Hispanic kid named Jesse from Dallas Metro and his family invited me to stay with them for a while. It felt like a good option because they lived close to Tia Licha and to Gabby. If I thought they needed a break for a night or two, there were places nearby I could stay. I liked having options so I wouldn't feel like a burden; plus, through all the years and anywhere I stayed, I always floated in and out of Gabby's to touch base with her and Alma. Well, that and do my laundry. I have SO many memories of walking down sidewalks with a garbage bag of dirty laundry, heading to Gabby's to wash it. Then I would pack my clean clothes into a new trash bag before Cesar got home and be gone again. She was always good to me through the years, but staying with her wasn't an option because of my past with Cesar.

Each time I bounced in or out of Tía Licha's house for a night, a week, a month, I would ask permission to stay, and each time, she would tell me I needed to ask her husband, my *tío*. They were family, and they were there for me, but this small action communicated to me that I wasn't automatically welcome; I needed to ask. My *tío* never said no, but his answers felt reluctant. The sense I got was they were going above and beyond, and I should be extremely grateful, which I was. I was thankful. I just wasn't home.

When I moved in with Jesse's family, I had the strangest conversation with my uncle. He told me, in kind of a harsh, gruff way, *'Toño, you can't be doing this. You can't be staying back and forth in all of these people's homes who aren't your family."* He said it like he was disgusted with me. I was so confused. I wanted to yell at him, "What do you think I'm doing? Do you think I like this? Do you have any other ideas?!" But I said nothing.

To this day, that conversation bewilders me. I felt like I was a burden to my aunt and uncle, to almost anyone. I was trying to manage, to handle, and to keep moving so no one would be put out with me. It was obvious my *tio* thought I was doing a poor job with my situation. I wonder what he thought would have been a good option?

CHAPTER TWENTY-NINE

BY JUAN

A Gift
Un Regalo

I WAS WALKING TO Jesse's house, the family from Dallas Metro that had allowed me to stay with them, from practice one day in August, right after summer football started back, before my senior year actually began. It was late afternoon. There was a white truck passing by very slowly, which, in that neighborhood, was never a good thing. I kept my head down and kept walking. It wasn't unusual in East Dallas to be grabbed: for your money, your shoes, your drugs, or just as a random act of violence or control. All I could think was *I hope they're not trying to pick me up,* so when the truck turned around and came back toward me, my heart started racing! Plans of escape, running into an alley, or finding one to duck into, or the shortest route to get away from whatever was about to happen darted through my mind. The streets teach kids to think this way. Your mind is always racing; there is always a plan of escape. Guards are never let down. Not ever.

The truck crept back to me, and a man rolled down his window and started asking me questions. *How you doing? Where you headed? Where you coming from?*

To this day, I can't fathom why I talked to him. Maybe I was nervous and didn't know what else to do. Maybe the Holy Spirit stopped me from running away. I'm not really sure how it happened, but I ended up in a conversation with this older white man, whom I had never seen before in my life, hanging out the window of his big white truck.

"So you play football? You're a receiver? Let me ask you this. If the cornerback tackles you in the middle of a catch, takes you out, and your spine cracks, that could end your life, right? At least, your life as you know it. If you die tomorrow on a football field or walking down the street like you are right now, where are you going? Would you go to Heaven or Hell?"

Somewhere in my mind I was thinking *WHAT?! This dude just rolled up on me and he's talking about death?! I'm seventeen years old. Why I gotta be thinking about death?!* But another part of me was entranced. I knew about God. I knew Jesus came to die on the cross for my sins, and it was by His grace I had been saved. I had learned enough from Dallas Metro, YWAM, and Trinity to have convictions about things that kept me from many temptations that could have easily ensnared me. But I wasn't clinging to the Lord. I wasn't living for Him. I had no authentic relationship with Him.

I did believe, and so I answered the strange man. "I would go to Heaven. I know Jesus came to die for me and give me life." I think my answer surprised him. He looked at me for a second, reached way over, and bent down to the floorboard of his truck. For a split second I freaked out in my mind again. *He could be reaching for anything! Does he have a gun? What is he doing?!* The rational side of my brain had already calmed down, realizing this man was harmless and just wanted to talk to me about football. Well, football and life and God and Hell and stuff. I was pretty sure he didn't have a gun at this point.

As he sat back up straight after reaching way over and picking something up off the floorboard, he handed a Bible out the window. 'Here. Keep this.' We talked for a few more seconds, maybe a few more minutes, but I can't tell you anything else that was discussed after that point. I only remember saying, "I hope we meet again sometime," as he pulled away. And I meant it.

Only moments before, I had thought this man was rolling up on me to jump me, to cause me harm. My interaction with him had shocked me, and almost nothing shocked me anymore. I continued walking down the street, chewing on the moment that had just passed. I looked down thinking, *What in the world was all that about?* I flipped the Bible open.

There was $140 inside of it! God's provision to me.

It was such a crazy moment. I walked the rest of the way home thanking God that He was real, that He was paying attention to me, and that He cared enough for me to orchestrate this meeting with a stranger!

I stuck ten percent of the money away immediately. I knew enough from YWAM and Dallas Metro to tithe, and the way the Lord provided this gift to me, I couldn't do anything except give back to Him his ten percent! I bought some football gloves, and I'm sure I went to the corner store and bought a few Monsters and Honey Buns because those were my favorite treats! Actually, I hate to admit it, but they kind of still are.

I have never seen that man again, but after all of these years, his gift is the Bible I still use. God gave me a gift through this man. Not just the $140, but also the moment that moved all the head knowledge I had learned from YWAM and Dallas Metro to my heart. I could not deny His love for me or the reality of the life He asks us to live.

My experience started a short season in my life where I began to journal. Maybe for the first time, I started spending alone time reading my Bible and praying like I had seen modeled for me, but had never done myself. I was getting acquainted with some of the youth at Trinity and realizing that teenagers could have deep knowledge of the Bible and of God all for themselves.

I was still staying with Jesse, and his family had a little patio area with a couch where I sat, read Scripture, and journaled. I started in the book of James. I would like to say it was because I'd heard it was one of the richest books on how to live the Christian life, but honestly, it was because it was one of the shortest! But that makes it no less powerful. God began to teach me lessons. *Consider it pure joy, my brothers, when you face trials of many kinds (James 1:2–3)* I had plenty of trials, but I began to think about looking at them through new eyes. I saw those around me who had true joy.

Let perseverance finish its work in you so that you may be mature and complete, not lacking anything (James 1: 4) I had always felt something inside of me telling me I was different, and that something had kept me from certain temptations, but I wasn't yet mature or complete. I still lacked many things that would help me stay the course, but I began watching the godly men around me to teach me how.

Be quick to listen, slow to speak and slow to become angry. (James 1:19) Every line I read was direct, true, relative to my life and circumstances, and was going to be key in leading me to let go of things from my past so that I could fully walk with God. I began to flip quickly to the right page when I went to youth group and Dustin called out a scripture. I began to be like some of those other kids I had watched and envied for knowing the Bible, for knowing God.

It was a sweet time of the Lord wooing me, where I first put in the effort to see who He really was. I encourage anyone reading my story right now to pick up a Bible and read James. New baby Christian or lifelong believer, the Word is true and powerful and sharper than any double edged sword and was breathed by the Holy Spirit to be our guide! To be an insight into the mind of Christ. To show us how to walk and where to go. Read it again. Chew on it. None of us can master any of its lessons fully on this side of Heaven, but our goal is to be more like Jesus, is it not? Let Him give you a gift today, just as he gave me through that man in the white truck years ago.

CHAPTER THIRTY
BY JUAN

A Whole New Scene
Una Nueva Escena

L ITTLE BY LITTLE, though it felt like overnight, the sweetness of this season with the Lord wore off. I was pulled away. It was football season, my senior year. I left Jesse's house. Nothing was wrong; I just had the normal feeling I'd been there too long, and it was time to go. They didn't have money either, and I didn't want to eat too much or strain them in any way. I had a friend from school I would stay with sometimes. His name was Anthony, and we played football together, so our schedules were the same, and that made it easy. If he had a ride, I had a ride, and the best part was...his mama cooked! She *always* cooked, and the food was good! I would crash on his couch, or stay with Gabby until Cesar and I got mad at each other again, then I would go back to Licha's for a few days.

I hung with Richie and my other church friends a lot less during my senior year, got a lot more involved in things at school, and began spending most of my time with new friends instead of going to Bible Study or a youth group. It wasn't a conscious choice; it seemed mostly a geographic decision, though I now know to be more watchful of subtle shifts in my heart. Spending less time at church, less time hearing Dustin and David speak truth to me, and less time around other kids who knew and loved God, made me open and vulnerable for hope to slip away. And it did.

It had been three years since my parents had left. Three years of surviving, house hopping, figuring out a way to survive. In the beginning, I was in shock and didn't really think about things. I guess I was waiting for my parents to come back, just biding my time until they returned. But now, being on my own had begun to wear on me. It was no longer 'my situation'… it was my life. It was a new way of thinking to sink in to the knowledge that I truly had no family, belonged nowhere, and the scene of my life that played over and over again was house hopping and survival. There were things about it and about myself that I had started to despise.

There were times I wanted to go to Anthony's, that he invited me to crash or just come hang out, but I had realized something. I hated the feeling I got when I wondered if someone would feed me or take care of me in some way. I would check myself, my motives, *am I going to Anthony's just to eat*? I didn't want to mooch or just show up for the food, even if it was being offered. I did the same thing with my cousin Gabby for years. I always kept in touch with them, even after Cesar kicked me out. I would drop by to visit, say hi to Alma, do laundry, and Gabby would feed me or give me 10 or 20 dollars. Gabby taking caring of me when I came by happened enough times that when I was desperate, the thought would pop in my mind, 'Hey, if I go visit, she might give me something.' I hated those kinds of thoughts! I hated being a kind of person that would have those thoughts, so sometimes I stayed away on purpose. I would stop myself from calling Gabby or going to Anthony's house just so I knew in my own gut that I wasn't a mooch.

There were new things going on my senior year that kept me going for a while. They changed the direction I was looking, focusing on something different than that recurring scene of my life. Mostly, I was hanging out with school friends. New friends. I also had a really cool

English teacher who poured into his students. His name was Mr. M, and I thought he was the smartest person I had ever met. I admired that; being smart felt strong to me. He used a lot of big words, and because I used to carry a dictionary, looking up every new word I heard and trying to expand my vocabulary for years, I liked that. He started a chess club so that we could all hang out with him after school. I had always thought chess was really boring, really geeky, and really white!! But I liked Mr. M, so I hung out and watched.

Eventually I even tried playing a little, and I must confess, I loved chess! It challenged me and felt like a workout for my mind. I was still in the mode that I wanted to distance myself from anything that felt ghetto, and what could be more opposite of ghetto than chess?!

By the end of my senior year, I had beaten Mr. M four times! Two of those times were because he was training me and let me take a turn back when I had made a mistake, but two of them were totally legitimate! I had not had many opportunities to think much of myself, didn't have a lot to be proud of, and thought I had no one to teach me anything new or anyone to tell me 'good job' when I learned it. Because I thought Mr. M was the smartest guy alive, beating him felt like such an accomplishment to me. To know that I could win a mind challenge really began to shift the way I thought about myself. I still have the journal where I recorded my victories!

So there were new things going on. The scenery around me looked different. Some good, some bad, but different. So I could pretend that meant things were changing, but underneath, it was the opposite. A deep storm, like the ones I knew earlier in my life, was brewing. I couldn't escape the fact that, no matter what I did, no matter how many activities I got involved in to distract myself that I was getting further and further away from having a family.

CHAPTER THIRTY-ONE
BY JUAN

Hello to Hopeless
Hola a Desesperados

FOOTBALL SEASON ENDED, and the invisible storm clouds shifted. I guess since we weren't at practice late, going home with some of my friends felt way more intrusive. I moved back in with Gabby for a little bit. Alma was back with her, and I was drawn to be anywhere that I could feel like I had a family, even though I knew before I even stepped foot in their apartment it wouldn't last long because nothing had changed with Cesar. We butted heads, and I could feel anger well up inside of me, which was something I tried to avoid at all costs. Whenever I felt my fists ball up or bit the inside of my lip to keep me from mouthing or saying something I might regret, I would remember Gabby saying to me years before, "So, you're gonna be just like your dad?!" I decided, after only a short time and several tense moments, to pack up again, knowing that if I stayed there with Cesar any longer, it would not turn out well.

I burned a hole in the sidewalk between Licha's, Anthony's, and other friends. I hardly went to church, I washed laundry at Gabby's, and I kept moving. I was exhausted and depressed. I had almost made it all of the way through high school, basically homeless and with no family, yet here it was, nearing the end of my senior year and I began to feel more hopeless than ever. I even joined in with the senior class as they started partying more and more, and I began drinking for the first time ever. Maybe the hopelessness was because I subconsciously realized that my one goal, finishing high school, was almost at hand and I had no idea what would become of me after that. Maybe it was just exhaustion. Whatever it was, it was dark and heavy. I began waking up as early as I could handle, just to get out of whatever house I was staying before anyone else woke up. I stayed out as long as I could, wandering the streets so I wouldn't have to face anyone.

I walked a lot. Alone. There was a particular stretch of road close to the high school that began to haunt me. At Fitzhugh and Central Expressway, I would cross the bridge and look out over cars down below. It made me think of a book I had read called *Tears of a Tiger*. A teenage kid looked over the edge of a bridge and said the cars looked like bullets whizzing by. The book was right; they did. I would pass that spot and look over the highway and think, *In just a few seconds, all of this pain could be over. I'm so tired of the struggle. I just want it to be over.* The kid in that book committed suicide. I had read about the effect his suicide had on his friends. The whole story blurred with mine and weighed heavy in my brain like a brick.

The thoughts of suicide became a daily mental struggle. I thought about the kid in the book as I crossed the bridge after school every day. I thought of things, like the look of disgust on my uncle's face, the disapproval. I felt the loneliness of having no family and nowhere to call home. I wrestled with hopelessness and heaviness. Every day, I longed for the fight to be over. I would make it across the bridge and think, *That's it. I'm done. I'm lying down and not getting up. I quit.*

But there was always this other feeling, this pushing or pulling, I'm not really sure what. *Get up. Keep going. You can do it. Don't quit.*

You're not alone, and you're not living this life just for yourself. You've got your parents, your brothers, your sisters. It was like a force, a rumbling, like someone was watching over me and keeping me safe, keeping me moving, though even with all of my head knowledge, and even with some of the miraculous gifts God had already given me, I still didn't get it. I still had no idea what this feeling was. I didn't know it was Him.

But I would get up, take another step, and do the whole thing again the next day.

CHAPTER THIRTY-TWO

BY JUAN

And then God Spoke
Y Dios Hablo

WEEK OR TWO before I graduated from high school, I got a craving to go to Monday Night Kid's Club at YWAM, which now that I look back was hypocritical because my friends and I were already making big drinking and partying plans for after graduation. I hadn't been to YWAM in quite a while, mostly because if we went to church, we went to Wednesday youth group at Trinity. I guess I wanted to go back and show off that I had made it. I needed something to feel good about. Trying to dig my way out of this hopelessness, I thought flaunting that I was a big, bad senior and that I was going to graduate might help. I asked Ralph, whom I hadn't seen in a while, if he wanted to go with me, and called good-ole faithful David to come pick us up.

We were bragging to everyone at Kid's Club about being grown and about graduating. I was using a bunch of new big words I'd been learning from studying the dictionary and hanging out with Mr. M. I guess I was feeling pretty good for a few minutes, but I was only fooling myself. I had just been able to chase away the torment for an hour by showing off how "great" I was doing. Then David, in his very soft hearted, non-threatening way, asked if they could pray for us.

It sounds ridiculous, but his question caught me off guard. I'd been around David for years. I'd been to Bible Studies and Kid's Club and Summer Church Camp. I should have expected him to pray for me, but I was so wrapped up in elevating myself to everyone there, the question shut me up. *Sure.* So they prayed blessings and wisdom over the next part of our lives after graduating, *blah, blah, blah.* Normal stuff. It was nice. Sweet. Generic. *Amen.*

The group started winding down, getting ready to leave, and chatting. Out of nowhere, a young woman, (I later learned her name was Emele), who was apparently volunteering with YWAM, approached me. She had no idea who I was, but she explained to me that she'd had an image pop into her mind while they were praying for me and asked if she could share it with me. What are you supposed to say to that? *Sure.*

Then, this perfect stranger proceeded to tell me that she saw me all alone, walking. She saw that I had no parents, no family, and that I was lost and wandering place to place, house to house, that I belonged nowhere. She saw that I had much pain and suffering and that my heart was weighed down with great sorrow. With so much hurt. She told me all of this heartache could only be melted by surrendering my life fully to God. She said she had seen my life in the image in her mind; she saw all of the past, all of the hopelessness and hurt, melting away and being turned into joy! Emele went on to say that she saw in my heart that I hated it when people were treated wrongly, especially women and that those feelings were from God and that He would use them for His purposes. I was amazed when she mentioned the anger I felt when I saw injustice and people being mistreated because I had never discussed that with anyone. I knew that God had to be speaking through her!

The image finished with me lifting weights and getting fit and strong, something that mattered to me a great deal, not wanting to be weak, playing football, wanting to be perceived as strong. Emele said these weights, this strength, was for me to be *both* physically fit and spiritually fit.

Then David took me home. I think I was so stunned I had no idea what to do with the whole experience. I wrote it all down, as if to try and process it again. It was like I had watched it happen, but it didn't happen to me.

I graduated a week later and went through with my partying plans. The Lord never left me, of course, but numbness had grown from hopelessness. I could feel God pursuing me, and I had known truth for years, but I was chewing on the image Emele had shared with me, trying to figure out how to get it from my head to melting my heart. In the meantime, I didn't want to "miss out" on anything. I was planning to go back to summer camp with Dallas Metro the next week. I figured I could get it all straightened out with God then and start over there.

But at camp, I met a girl. Isn't it always a girl?!

Her name was Gabriela, and she was a Christian. That was good for me, right? We started 'dating,' but she lived in Tyler, about 100 miles from Dallas, so it was a long distance thing, I guess. A long distance thing with me, who had no money and no car. However, we talked a lot on the phone, and I was smitten. She was the first girlfriend I was really into and that I thought could really be something.

Mr. M, that cool English teacher I'd had my senior year, taught me how to drive a stick shift and actually let me borrow his car to go visit her in Tyler! I don't know what he was thinking, but I took him up on it! I had graduated. I had a girlfriend. I took several trips back and forth to visit her over the next few months. It was a great summer...

Except for this one thing, I don't want to call anyone out, so I won't mention names, but part of that summer, I would wake up on this particular couch, in this particular friend's house I was crashing in...itchy! Skin crawling! On fire! Uncomfortable! After time, I realized that couch had bed bugs! So when Ralph and Tall Richie got an apartment on their own, and a counselor from the high school got me a twin bed through a certain program for kids trying to make it, I asked if I could put my bed in their apartment.

There was this closet space just exactly big enough, *only* exactly big enough, to squeeze a twin mattress between the walls and have a tiny floor space to stand up. That became my room, and I hung a curtain over the opening. It was in that tiny closet space, on that twin mattress, where the image Emele had shared with me played out. It was where the act of surrendering to God, giving Him all of my pain and sorrow, actually became a reality.

CHAPTER THIRTY-THREE

BY JUAN

Surrender
Rendición

IT STARTED WITH a break up, as many life-changing situations do. The entire summer I had desperately been trying to ignore the hopelessness and depression that were fighting so hard to overtake me. My head had peeked out from behind the clouds for a few months, and I almost thought I would make it. I easily stayed away from that bridge now, since I wasn't walking home from school every day. The summer had begun with house hopping and had ended with me actually having a bed, in a sort-of, kind-of, room of my own. I was the first and only high school graduate in my family! I had a girlfriend. Life should have been better. But I began to notice Gabriela didn't seem to act the same with me, and I wondered if our relationship was coming to an end.

Then I got a text saying she wasn't ready for a relationship. A text! Seriously? Who does that?! Oh, the woes of teenage dating and modern technology! I was devastated. I threw the phone on the bed and left the house. I needed a walk, a long walk, and the heaviness I'd been trying to ignore rushed back in, more overwhelming than ever.

Dating Gabriela felt like one of the only things I had going for me, and she'd ended it with a text. I kept walking. Somewhere, about an hour in to the walk—that heaviness turned into a prayer. *God, I'm tired of this. I'm so tired of this. I can't do it anymore. I need it to be over.* I kept walking, but steered away from bridge. I couldn't handle the temptation.

For a few weeks, Gabriela and I still talked off and on. She had said we could still be friends, giving me hope we would work things out before I started community college in Dallas, at El Centro. She even asked me to come back to Tyler to visit one more time before summer was over. I daydreamed all the way there of conversations we would have, cementing our feelings for one another and starting over. I thought for sure I'd start college with her as my girlfriend! I thought for sure that the betrayal and hurt of the past few weeks was over, and everything was going to be okay... until I drove all the way there to hang out with all of our mutual friends, like she'd asked me to, and she wasn't there to meet me. Until I had to wait half an hour for her to show up. Until she showed up with another guy and barely paid attention to me.

I felt so rejected. What had happened? Why had she asked me to visit? Why had God let our relationship happen? Like I needed one more reason to feel left or abandoned!

I returned to Dallas a heavy heap. Through friends and a small scholarship I was starting community college the next day, something I never thought would happen. But I didn't even care. All of the hurt and pain, the sorrow from the image Emele had seen, all of it came to a head. I hid in my little closet room, face down on the bed, listened to worship music on the radio, and cried. I clung to every word of those lyrics like they were my only life line, the only thing keeping me off the edge of that overpass. Soon, I began turning them all into prayers. "Everyone needs compassion, the kindness of a Savior, let mercy fall on me."[8]

---

8   *Mighty to Save*—song by Hillsong Music

I'm tired of feeling alone, God.

"Everyone needs forgiveness, the kindness of a Savior, the hope of nations."

I'm tired of feeling hopeless. Please forgive me for thinking I can ignore you and keep trying things my own way.

"So take me as you find me, all my fears and failures, fill my life again. I give my life to follow everything I believe in. Now I surrender."

I'm tired of going from house to house, place to place, belonging nowhere, having nothing to eat. My way is not working. I surrender.

Emele Falahola, YWAM Dallas full time volunteer. The "perfect stranger" who spoke that image over Juan, and then years later they are working together at YWAM.

"My Savior, you can move the mountains. My God is Mighty to save. He is mighty to save. Forever, Author of salvation, He rose and conquered the grave. Jesus conquered the grave!"

I worshipped for hours in that little closet room. I sobbed. I surrendered. And over the hours, a weight lifted, and I heard the Lord speak to me. Not an audible voice, but in my spirit, and it was no less real. It said, "Do not worry about it son. Just lay it all down. Follow my path."

It was exactly the picture God had given Emele to share with me months before. Surrender melted the sorrow away from my heart. I woke up the next morning feeling lighter. Life wasn't easier overnight, and I still had a long way to go, but I have never been the same since that night. I have never again looked down on cars whizzing by and thought, "I just need it to be over." I have never felt that hopeless again. Not since I surrendered.

CHAPTER THIRTY-FOUR

BY JUAN

Two Miracles
Dos Milagros

STARTING COLLEGE WAS a miracle. Part of the hopelessness during my senior year of high school had been wondering what I could do with my life after graduation. Kids all around me at school were talking about college plans, scholarships, and entrance essays; I tuned their conversations out. I knew the school counselors were working with kids all the time to get them financial aid, help them choose colleges, and so forth, but I was afraid to even ask. Because of my illegal immigrant status, I assumed college was out of the question. I was so tired of feeling shunned and rejected; I couldn't bear getting my hopes up for college and then being told no. I was also afraid to ask. Going to a counselor and explaining my situation could cause problems of all kinds. I was so used to keeping my head down, not drawing attention to myself, afraid that if anyone noticed me, it would cause problems. I was still a minor with no guardian, and I was illegal.

Finally, though, I figured I had no other options and nothing to lose by looking into going to college. I heard about this program that helped kids apply for scholarships, get financial aid, and prepare them for college. I started asking around and realized it was a deal students had been involved in since 10th grade! I'm sure I was told about it at school, but tuned it out or something, assuming it wasn't a possibility for me. But I was so desperate at this point, I went to my high school counselor, let's call her Ms. Gonzalez, to ask.

Ms. Gonzalez actually worked for a non-profit foundation, which I will not name, that served out of North Dallas High School. They placed counselors in the high school to inform kids of their programs, track them through high school, and prepare them for college. As soon as I met Ms. Gonzalez, she was wonderful to me! Walking into her office was one of the best choices I've ever made. I told her everything, things I had been afraid to tell anyone in any position of authority about my situation. She didn't blink an eye or react with shock or disapproval. She just jumped in to start helping me apply for college and financial aid. The paperwork, essays, applications... she helped me with all of it. I got accepted to a few different schools, but El Centro gave me a scholarship called Rising Star. I received money toward books and tuition, and I enrolled!

Going to college was a miracle, something I never thought possible! Not during my days of roaming the streets and pulling pranks with Fat Richie, not through all of the financial struggles of my family, not since I learned what it meant to be an illegal immigrant, and that I *was* one, and definitely not since being left in America with no family and no support. I was going to be a college student!

I also began off and on attending a men's Bible Study led by Scott Robson, a man from Trinity who became a great example of how to seek after the deep knowledge of God, and who began to walk beside me as a mentor. I watched him and learned from him, and he blessed me tremendously during this season. He even bought me my very first pair of glasses, which I had needed since middle school but never had the resources to purchase!

As I came back to the Lord and went further and further into His love for me, I had so many people loving me, walking with me, and

Scott Robson and Juan

teaching me. I was at the Trinity Youth Group with Dustin again on a regular basis. Scott had told me to text if I ever wanted to go to Bible Study Saturday mornings. I had been a few times before, but now every Saturday I texted, and every Saturday he picked me up and poured into me. He would drop whatever he was doing anytime to show up for me in whatever way I needed—prayer, advice, or groceries.

I also stayed in contact with Ms. Gonzalez after graduation. She helped me with so many things. She even helped me get a bed when I moved into the closet room! I would visit her at the non-profit head-quarters office after classes at El Centro. I started spending a lot of time there, and everyone in that office was so willing to help me with my academics and anything else I was struggling with. They began tending to me, asking me about my day, if I needed help with anything, what I was learning, if I needed groceries. They began functioning as my support system. Then another opportunity arose, something else I had wanted for a long time and never thought I'd have.

My sister Alma's experience of being left in America was very different than mine. Like I said before, she had more steady living situations. Not having a home with parents was still very difficult for her, just different. She always worked. She babysat, even moved in with a family as their nanny who eventually wanted to adopt her. She cleaned with a friend's mom. Whatever she could do, whatever it took, she did. *Chispa*—little spark. She was a go-getter and was always able to find income. I never did, not officially, just side jobs here and there.

The same fear and hopelessness I had about trying to explain my situation and applying for college rose up in me whenever I thought about getting a job. I'd do work on the side here or there for a friend's dad who would pay me in cash, but I never had anything legit. To have a legitimate job, I needed a social security card, and that was something I didn't have. It was another area of life where I was shut down, afraid to want, afraid to ask, and tired of hearing, 'No.' Fear, worry, isolation, not included or belonging. A feeling of being on the outside of the system. All of these were collateral damage of being an illegal immigrant in America.

But Ms. Gonzalez and the ladies who worked at this non-profit organization changed all that. They worked out some way of paying me off the record, gave me a job, and became even more a daily part of my life. They were the closest thing I'd had to a daily family unit in a long time. They encouraged me, asked me about my day, helped me get things I needed, such as pots, pans, and even a computer for school! They gave me dignity and allowed me to hold my head up high.

I had already experienced God's miracles in my life—a job and a chance at a college education—but it was during the two years I worked for this organization, after surrendering my life to Jesus in that little closet room and after starting school, that I was truly filled with passion for the Lord. I attended Trinity, soaked in as much as I could from anyone there, followed Dustin and Scott around to learn from them, and served in any way I knew how. I was doing street ministry downtown every weekend, feeding the homeless with a group from YWAM, going on any mission trip I heard about, working, and going to school.

Life was busy and full, but I was driven by this new relationship I had with God. I wanted everyone to know and experience the surrender, the hope, and the love. I couldn't get enough of seeing God move.

When new management took over at work, I knew that my time was limited. I felt it, figuring the new leadership would not allow the same agreement to pay me off the record. The Lord was kind enough to give me a sense of peace about leaving that job before it even happened. I felt like He told me they were going to let me go, and within a week, I was. It had been such a neat season where I learned so much and received so much support that I couldn't be upset at all, especially since being let go freed me up for more ministry, the direction my life seemed to be going in the first place!

Those two opportunities did so much for my view of myself, as well as my vision for life. It was a miracle to me that I had the chance to receive a college education, and that, even when facing my fears and explaining my situation out loud to people, God had provided. I knew He was on my side, and I was going places!

Juan praying for this man while doing street ministry in downtown Dallas.

CHAPTER THIRTY-FIVE

BY JUAN

Dustin

I WAS EIGHTEEN YEARS old before I shaved for the first time. I didn't know when most teenage guys started shaving. No one ever talked to me about it until I was at Dustin's house one night, and he said, "What's up with those two chin hairs sticking out like an antennae? It's time for you to shave, boy!" Monica, Dustin's wife, swatted at him, fussing about his direct way. He shrugged his shoulders and said, "What? Someone's gotta tell him!" Needless to say, I began shaving shortly after that.

As I began watching Dustin and trying to mirror the qualities I saw in him, he taught me many lessons in both the natural and in the spiritual. I'd known men of God before—Pastor Clay and David Funke, but I was at a different stage in my life when I met them. They were quiet, faithful men who poured into me as I drifted in and out of their paths. I hadn't yet been watching for lessons on living life as a godly man.

I had already known Dustin for a while when I became ready for these lessons. I still thought I would have to teach myself, just like the words I made myself study so I could hopefully be perceived in a different way. But this one particular time, in Dustin's office, God showed me another way to learn.

Trinity Church Youth Pastor Dustin Sample and Juan, 2011.

I thought I was doing great, making good choices, doing a fine job of turning myself over to God. It was after they had let me go from work, and I wanted to attend a Discipleship Training School through YWAM, so I was asking Dustin for guidance and help in raising support. I can't even remember the circumstances, but I must have been saying something opposite of what he had advised me, or I must have done something he had cautioned against. I just remember him leaning across his desk, kinda slapping his hand down and saying, "Listen to your daddy! Do what I told you."

I was stunned. I just sat there and stared at him. I thought no one had taken responsibility for me in a long time. I still didn't understand the spiritual family that had been offered to me. My father had been gone for years at this point. Even before he was sent back, he wasn't someone who spoke into my life with wisdom or out of concern for my best. 'Daddy' was a term of affection, of endearment. It connotes trust, love, and care. And it made me angry when he used it. I wanted to jump out of my chair and yell, 'Man, you ain't my daddy!' But I just stayed quiet and stared back at him.

It took me a long time to process what Dustin had said. I'd had women refer to themselves as Mama types in my life. I was able to accept that. They tended to me, fed me, and hugged me, and I desperately needed that. I could see God wanting to love me, take care of me, hug me, and be tender to me like a mom. For some reason, that kind of love was easy for me. It was familiar. I'd actually had that type of relationship with my mother, but I never remember having a daddy. My dad had mostly spoken into my life out of anger, and Cesar had tried to boss me, control me in the same way, out of drunkenness and anger. Eggshells. Volcanoes waiting to erupt. That's what I thought of when I thought of fathers. I knew God was my father, and that he was a perfect father. I just wasn't sure what that looked like.

Trinity Youth Paster, Dustin Sample's family. His wife Monica, daughter Addison, and son Noah.

Until Dustin sought me out. He made himself, his family, and his life available to me. I watched the way he did things, and he watched me. He knew I needed a father figure, and he stepped into that role in a mighty way. He's pretty small in stature, but the stance he took in my life was not. Watching Dustin's life was such a different way for me to view a man.

I was able to see Dustin as a leader during youth group and as a father and husband at his home with his family. I saw that he was a loving papa to his two children. I saw how their family operated in trust, with him as the covering. I even witnessed small disagreements between him and Monica, his wife. I had NEVER seen a healthy marriage in my life, so when they had a disagreement in front of me, I thought, 'uh oh... here it comes,' but they handled it totally different than anything I'd ever seen before. Seeing him in all of these roles taught me I could trust him, as a man and as a father figure, and this example led to me view God in a different way... as my Father.

I remembered God speaking to me in that little closet room. He had said, 'Do not worry about it, *son*. Lay it all down and follow my path.' The words were tender and loving, but also gave guidance, direction, the same way Dustin had spoken to me. That experience in his office when he told me to "listen to daddy" changed my relationship with him. It also changed my relationship with the Lord, and it gave me a glimpse of God as my Father. It opened a crack in my heart to see the family that was being offered to me through relationships at Trinity. I began to understand that when people offered me relationship, they were offering family.

The years Dustin walked beside me laid a foundation for the new spiritual house I'm living in today. I would not have learned how to make my life a dwelling place for God, or relate to Him as my Father were it not for Dustin.

CHAPTER THIRTY-SIX
BY JUAN

The Hand of God
La Mano de Dios

A<small>S I TRULY SURRENDERED</small> more and more to God, as that crack in my heart got bigger and bigger, and I saw a family forming around me, I found myself walking more and more in relationship with people. I stopped jumping around so much. I went to school, I worked, and I became very involved in ministry at YWAM and Trinity. I began to open up my life to men like Dustin and Scott and began watching them, and for the first time, I began having real thoughts of what I needed to do to be a godly man. They read the Bible. They knew the Bible, and they knew their God. They expected God to move, they asked God to move, and they saw God move. Then they shared their faith with people, so I began to mirror them. I began expecting God to move and asking Him to move. I had only pretty much prayed when things got bad in my life. That began to change.

I prayed that my parents could have a place of their own in México to live instead of staying with relatives. I prayed they would have the strength to get off drugs. I prayed they would have a reliable phone, so I could call them to talk whenever I wanted. These things began to happen. I prayed, and I saw God move. What I was experiencing was incredible!

I will never forget the first time I prayed with my parents on the phone. I was talking to them one time, and Dad, who was clean and sober for the first time in quite a while, was complaining about not having any work and worrying what they were going to do. His life sounded so helpless and hopeless to me. I didn't know what else to do, so I told him to stop worrying and to stop complaining. We needed to pray.

I closed my eyes to talk to God. All of a sudden, I realized I had never prayed in Spanish. The churches I went to had always been in English, and the words didn't want to come out in Spanish. I began stuttering and thought I'd made a mistake so boldly asking my parents to join me in prayer. Then something happened. Prayer started pouring out of me in Spanish. I heard the words, and I knew what I was saying, but they weren't my words. I wasn't even thinking those thoughts; they were just there and coming out. I closed my eyes tight and had the most incredible sensation of flying, floating. I felt like I was in the room with my parents, like we were all there together praying. I even had to open my eyes a few times during the prayer to make sure my feet were on the ground.

When I said, "Amen," I told my dad, "I feel like someone is going to call you and offer you a job. Soon. I feel like God is saying it's gonna happen." Praying like this was a bold thing for me. Not only did I not hear God speak to me very often, but also I knew there was no work in Juárez. I knew it was almost impossible for my dad to find a job, but I also knew God was moving and stirring my faith and teaching me how to step out and believe.

A few days later, I called to check on my parents and my dad reported that someone had called, and he had a job! Things like this just propelled me forward in my walk with God. He cared about me. He heard me. He spoke to me, and he followed through on His word. After so many years of hopelessness and defeat, it was so awesome to me to have this knowledge!

CHAPTER THIRTY-SEVEN

BY JUAN

Music
Música

FROM A YOUNG age, I loved rap, I loved lyrics, and I truly believed words have power. I was about fifteen when the vision for music was first planted in me. I was out in the neighborhood with Dallas Metro. They used an empty lot in the neighborhood to set up regular programs every weekend and sometimes on Thursday nights outside, in the neighborhood with the people. They had just begun packing up the truck, and I was just hangin' out when all of a sudden, things started to move in slow motion in my mind. I looked around and as I did, it was like a scene from a movie. I stood there on that empty lot and did a full circle, turning slowly and looking around at the ghetto, at the kids, at the crappy, dirty, hopeless neighborhood. I heard God's voice inside me say, "I want you to rap my Word." Then the movie scene ended.

I believed what I heard was God speaking to me, but I was immature spiritually. I thought it made me cool, and I started telling everyone at Dallas Metro that I was going to be a Christian rapper. Trouble was, I couldn't write. I would sit down and start trying my

Juan performing at the Church of Living Hope, Tyler, TX, 2011

hand at lyrics, but I couldn't get past one line. I would quit, but the idea, that movie scene, that voice I heard, never left me. I tried a year later to sit down and write. But nothing. A year after that, nothing. But I never forgot.

It wasn't until after I fully surrendered to God that I started hearing that voice again. Every time I thought of it, I would see that same scene play out in my head from that empty lot: the ghetto, the hopelessness, and the voice. 'I want you to rap my Word.' I was listening to a lot of Christian rap at the time. Lecrae and 116 Clique, and their lyrics influenced me. They encouraged me. They convicted me. There was even a Lecrae song I used to skip all of the time because it would so stir up conviction in me and I couldn't face it. But as I began walking more closely with the Lord, and learned that mercy triumphed over judgment, I knew it was His kindness that led me to conviction, and I would listen to the song and be broken all over again.

When I started learning the Bible during youth group at Trinity, I realized a lot of the lyrics in the Christian rap I listened to were scripture. I had known they were about God, but when I started reading scripture I recognized them as straight from God's Word, so I began to rap scripture in my head as I read it. I would learn a new verse and it would resonate as a rap in my heart. Still, I felt like there was more... that God had a message He wanted me to convey in my own words.

I finally decided that I didn't care if I sucked. I was going to write. Little by little, the words began to come. One of the first complete songs I wrote was a theme song for VIBE, the youth group at Trinity.

I had been working on it, and one morning I woke myself up rapping in my sleep. I was crashed out on Gabby's couch and I could have sworn it was flowing out of me in my sleep, but I thought I might have been dreaming. I asked Gabby if she had heard anything and she said, "Yes, I heard you practicing." Rapping in my sleep began happening a lot. I would wake up rapping. I realized the lyrics weren't my words. God was giving them to me, and they were flowing out while I wasn't even awake! They were coming from a place that wasn't me.

Juan performing at YWAM Dallas, 2013

I told Dustin what was going on and asked him if I could rap my song at VIBE during youth group. Mind you, Dustin didn't know me very well at this point, so he was a bit reluctant. However, he let me. It was the first time I'd ever rapped in front of people! And it was my own song! It was fine, I guess, but I ran out of breath. It was a learning experience for me. I realized there was more skill to rapping than lyrics or being cool. Like so many other things, I can look at my first songs and see the immaturity. But that caused me to see my growth as a rapper, my spiritual growth, and my growth as a man.

Rapping is fun, and I love it, but it's not just something I do. There have been men I have watched and learned from. There have been people that walked with me for a season and spoke pieces of truth into my life, but there has never been one man who took me by the hand as I left boyhood and stepped fully into my life who said, 'Here, walk this way,' on a daily basis, day after day, year after year. But the music did. That's why it's more than music to me. It took me by the hand.

Juan performing at Dallas Metro Summer Camp, 2009.

Juan performing at Dallas Metro Summer Camp, 2012.

It spoke truth, it discipled. It convicted me, brought me close to God, and kept me there. I knew as a teenager that words have power. Proverbs 18 was one of the first Bible Studies I remember. *The power of life and death is in the tongue.* I had a choice between speaking blessings and speaking curses. That's what music is to me. Lecrae and 116 Clique, their songs still resonate. They still push me, bless me, and hold me accountable.

Because God has moved more and more in my life and because I have seen him save me in many, many ways, I want to tell everyone. I want everyone to experience and know God like I have had the great privilege of doing. If He would use my music to speak that message, well, that's just about the greatest thing I could imagine.

CHAPTER THIRTY-EIGHT

BY JUAN

Healing and Home
Sanación y Hogar

A T SOME POINT, Alma moved back in with Gabby. Gabby's daughter, who was teeny tiny when I had lived with them before, was now a full-blown kid. I was there one day, hanging out and doing laundry, when she looked at me and said, *"Toño, why don't you come back and live with us?"* People wanting me around so much that they would ask me to stay wasn't the norm for me, but it warmed me being there, like a family. I loved the idea. We asked Cesar, and he gave the okay, though I'm sure he was reluctant because any time I had stayed with them for even the shortest amount of time, he and I had friction. This time would be different, though, whether he knew it or not, because I was different.

Whenever I had been there before, for many years, even before the night he kicked me out, I'd felt tension with Cesar. I had felt so much hatred from him that it made me want to hate him back. He had this mole! I used to even hate the sight of it! But that anger had been melted by the Lord. The tension was gone from my heart, and that created a totally different atmosphere in the apartment. Everything was different this time around.

Juan working at YWAM activity center, 2014

This was actually the point at which my family—Alma, Gabby, even Cesar—really saw that God had changed me. They had only known the defensive me, on eggshells, snapping and fighting with Cesar. Other than that, I had only floated in and out for years to do laundry or crash for a night. They all commented on this new softness, the new attitude surrounding my heart. I tried inviting them to church, but Gabby was always working, and I think Cesar controlled her in ways similar to how Pa used to control Ma, so she only came once or twice, and Alma, who had always been the one dragging everyone to church, had changed.

Like me, she'd been on her own for years at this point, and she had her own story of survival, depression, hopelessness, and hanging on, and I think it hardened her. It would harden anyone. She has become guarded over the years. She is so amazing and strong, such a go-getter. My parents call her *Chispa*. Little spark. And she is. That has never changed, but other things in her have grown tired.

I remember feeling like the Lord had given me a picture for Alma. I told her about it, getting teary while trying to express God's love for her and this picture of a special gift God showed me that He has just for Alma. It's big, and all she had to do was reach out and get it.

Juan working with YWAM volunteer Ofa Falahola (Emile's husband) on the roof of the YWAM Dallas home.

I was new at hearing from the Lord, and I'm sure I didn't deliver the message in the best way, but to me, I was excited for her, and it was a loving word. She, however, took it as judgment from her big brother, as disapproval. *'Why aren't you reaching for it, Alma?'* I was so motivated to share what God had done in me and for me and driven to bring people to the Lord, it was heartbreaking to not be able to share it with my family at that time, but I have learned that is up to the Father. He loves them more than I could ever love them, and one day, they will take hold of Him because He has already taken hold of them.

Though I was disappointed about not being able to share much spiritually with my family, this time of living with them was still quite healing. It was such a different experience, especially between Cesar and me.

It was a super busy time. I was in school, serving at YWAM, going downtown on the weekends to talk about God's love to people on the streets, traveling on mission trips a lot, and being discipled as much as I could from Dustin and Trinity. But I had changed since living with them the last time. I knew many frustrations when it came to Alma or me living with them stemmed from keeping the house in order, and

Juan (in pulse t-shirt) working with Ellen Aragay, Alan Dorado, and Jose Carrillo, the Dallas YWAM group in Moore, Oklahoma after the 2013 tornado, helping repair the damage.

I wanted to contribute. I wanted to do my part, so I tried to be aware: wash dishes, take out the trash, do things without having to be asked or told, like my uncle had taught me. There were even a few times during this season when it was just Cesar and I at home alone. We hung out, played video games, and had some conversations.

In one of these conversations, Cesar very calmly suggested that I think about contributing to the house in different ways. His example was, 'Maybe like bring a gallon of milk home every once in a while.' It was so different than before. I was really trying to help around the house, and I'm sure he saw my efforts. He wasn't angry. He was just mentioning it. Looking back, Cesar was very young when Alma and I moved in. He had a young daughter, and he and Gabby struggled. It was a huge responsibility for them to take care of us, and I have no idea how they did it, so when he asked me for a gallon of milk, I took it to heart. I wanted to be respectful; to do my part. One day, I had a few bucks from a side job, and I stopped on the way home to buy a gallon of milk. I don't think anyone was home; it didn't matter. I remember opening the fridge and putting that gallon in there. I just stood there with the door open, looking at it. I felt like I had conquered the world!

It was a good time. I felt like I had a home. I didn't have to bounce around or wonder where I was going to sleep. I wasn't there a lot because there was so much going on between school, work and ministry, but when I was, I was at peace. I was learning,

Juan working in Joplin, Missouri with tornado relief, Arts With A Mission (AWAM), 2012.

growing, and hearing God. Then, as is typically the case with the Lord, He did something I didn't expect; He moved me again.

Through a series of conversations with Dustin, I began to think about the idea of living in a place that could pour into me spiritually. I was doing a lot of ministry at the time, and going home to a place of peace, but I wasn't being fed spiritually at home. I was no longer a boy; I was becoming a man, and I certainly had lots to learn about what that meant. Dustin spoke with David Funke, sharing his concern that I needed to build on everything the Lord was doing in my life so that I wouldn't get burned out, so that I would continue to grow and mature as a man of God. David took what Dustin was telling him to heart, chewed on it for a few days, and by the time I spoke to him, he offered me a place to live at the YWAM house. A home.

Living at YWAM has been the longest I have lived anywhere in my entire life.

I'm so grateful that after years of house hopping, of trying to avoid my rage for Cesar, that God provided this totally different experience.

Juan and Debbie Blair installing the new Jesus picture at YWAM Dallas, 2014.

It was so healing to be there with the last few pieces of family I had tried to cling to and be at peace. I think my finding a permanent place to live was healing for all of us. It was also healing to move from there in a totally different way. It was the first and only time I ever remembered moving because I chose to and not because I was running or being kicked out of an apartment with my family because we couldn't pay the bills, or because I was a burden and needed to go. Everything was good. There was no strife. I just chose something different because I heard God speak.

It was then that I realized that God, my Father, had *completely* transformed my life. I wasn't running. I was receiving. I wasn't a burden. I had a chance to be a blessing. I wasn't on survival mode or sad or lonely, or lost, or wandering. I had joy. I had spiritual family. I had options. I had peace, and was getting to make choices, instead of reacting to circumstances outside my control.

I had healing. I was not left alone.

I had a home.

PART FIVE

Lunch with the Redeemed
Almuerzo con los Redimidos

" In Him, we have redemption through his blood, the forgiveness of our trespasses, according to the riches of his grace."
Ephesians 1:7

"En Él tenemos redención por su sangre, el perdón de nuestros pecados según las riquezas de su gracia"
Efesios 1:7

CHAPTER THIRTY-NINE

BY SALLY

Reality Check
Verificación de la Realidad

IN THE SPARSE home of Juan's parents, I sat and talked for several hours with Juan Sr., Aurora, Nena and her two children, and Isaac (Juan's youngest brother). Aurora remained on the edge of the couch, holding my hand. Tears sat in her eyes most of the time we talked. They were so gracious, sending Isaac to the little store up the road to bring me a coke, even though I insisted I was comfortable and didn't need anything, telling funny stories about all of the kids when they were young, and opening their hearts and their home to me.

After a while, I asked if I could use the restroom and was told it was up the steep, narrow staircase that climbed the wall. At the top of the stairs, a sheet hung from an open place in the wall. I guess you would call it a doorway, though wider than that, and there was no door. The sheet was pushed back and the 'room' was in view. A mattress on the floor filled up almost the entire space, and a few worn out blankets were piled on top of it. The bathroom was tiny, all of the bulbs and electrical wire were exposed, and an extension cord had

Juan and his brothers, Isaac and Luis, reunited in El Paso TX. December 2011 for the first time in 7 years.

been strung up the wall from somewhere out of view, dangling loosely from the ceiling. This was the only source of electricity I saw anywhere upstairs.

They discussed with me the financial side of living in Juárez. Their apartment was actually owned by someone else, but it had been abandoned. They explained that living in an abandoned home was typical in Juárez. Whole buildings are run down, abandoned, trashed and left behind. Forgotten. Families or individuals who used to own them have fled Juárez in years past out of fear for their lives or at the onset of destitution. Squatters moved in to buildings, some as gangsters and dope heads and some as families, all looking for a safe dwelling place. Juan and Aurora had actually met the owners who came through town at one point; they were glad to see a family residing there because that meant it couldn't be used as a haven for drugs or prostitution. Apparently, if proof of good intentions can be provided, they could somehow get electricity and running water, and that was their hope. Until then, they had the draping extension cords, rigged up from some outside source of power.

Juan Sr. discussed work, that a full work week there is considered 60 hours. It is unheard of for the normal resident to have that much work available; he could almost never find work. Even if miraculously there happened to be a full week of work available, he would only have the opportunity to earn up to $40, a week. That's it, and that is unheard of. I do not consider myself to be sheltered, unexposed, even very shockable, but many of the things they spoke about were impossible to wrap my head around. The level of destitution in Juárez was one of those things.

Another was the danger. Luis, Juan's oldest younger brother, had recently joined Juan and Alma in the United States. Being an American citizen, he had no trouble re-entering the U.S, except, of course, that he was sixteen and leaving his parents. Luis now resides with Juan, and he and Alma co-parent their younger brother. When questioning the parents about their decision to send Luis to America, they explained that he was coming to the end of his education opportunities in Juárez, they wanted him to continue in school, and he was in more and more danger each day he remained. I thought my Spanish had failed me as Juan Sr. expressed the fear he had felt, knowing Luis wanted to be outside with his friends, but they worried because of the—he held both his hands up as guns, much like a kid playing cowboys and Indians might—and made the sound of an AK-47. 'Da-da-da-da-da.' He mimicked bullets.

"Oh," I said, "people would drive by shooting at night?" *At night, first thing in the morning, middle of the afternoon. The danger is everywhere.* For a split second, I felt afraid. I looked at the translator and thought, "Oh, good! He's talking about how any time, day or night, right outside their door, machine guns are present and fired. What have I gotten us into?" I looked around the room at Nena's children—six and three years old—and was overwhelmed imagining their futures. If they can face living with this fear every day, surely I could choke back fear for twelve hours. I didn't give my fear a second thought until now, as I type the story of my trip, in my comfortable home in Texas where I am free, lights come on when I flip a switch,

I have an education, I expect that my children will also, and I receive a paycheck.

Even now, while typing about what I learned on my trip to Juárez, my heart aches for Juan Sr. and Aurora. A few months after my visit, Isaac, being a citizen (since he was born in Texas), moved to Dallas to live with Juan and Luis at the YWAM house, so I do not have to ache for them. But my heart breaks for Nena, mostly for her children, sweet little faces that live in that reality. It is almost more than I can bear.

Juan's older sister Nena and her children in Juarez, Mexico.

CHAPTER FORTY

BY SALLY

God Bless the U.S.A.
Que Dios Bendiga a los Estados Unidos

I WAS PLEASANTLY SURPRISED with how open Ma and Pa Terrazas were. My worries about them being hesitant to share melted away immediately, for they not only reported everything I needed to hear to complete my story, but also they expressed many things I had not expected.

They sat with me all day, looking old beyond their ages because of a hard life, worry, and drug and alcohol abuse, but whenever they laughed, which was a lot during our time together, their eyes lit up, and they appeared as school aged children. I mentioned earlier that I felt I needed to see which emotions showed on their faces when they were asked about leaving their children, about the past. If I were given only one word to assign what shone through the surface, I would have to say "regret." Deep, aware, resigned regret. Not in a way that made them hopeless, but in a way of embracing the full knowledge of what they had done, how their choices led to where they are, and making absolutely no excuses for themselves. Not one.

I guess I expected a little more along the lines of, "Well, it was a hard time. We did the best we could, and we made some mistakes."

What I got instead was full confession. "The world and the devil are powerful, and I got sucked in. I was a drunk, I did crack, and I neglected my family." One precious moment, Juan Sr., who is not Nena's biological father, said, "We owe a lot to Nena. It fell to her to take care of the kids when we didn't. She held it all together. I always want to thank her for that."

Nena just looked at the floor in a way that showed she acknowledged, and there was forgiveness, but years of pain and feeling alone had already taken their toll. Now, those she took care of when no one else would—Juan, Alma, Luis—were in the United States with more hope than she had ever known while she sat there, in the living room, in dirty Juárez, with her parents and me. They showed gratitude for Nena.

And they showed gratitude that the Lord has sustained them, that He saved them, that He has not allowed them to perish, to die in the absolute mess and iniquity they created, that they are clean and sober now, and that part of their family is in America and has hope. There was only remorse when discussing the United States and how they wasted their opportunity. No blame or anger over the arrest or deportation. *La cosa que me encanta de América es...la ley, es la ley.* "The thing I love about America is, the law is the law," Juan, Sr. said. "You can't buy it or change it." *Aqui, todo es corruptado. Si tienes, puedes cambiar la ley.* "Here, everything is corrupt. If you have," and he held out a hand with a thumb and pointer finger, as if to show off a huge wad of cash, "you can change the law. And if not..." He swiped his hands together as if to brush off the dirt and shrugging his shoulders, said, "Oh well, then."

I didn't expect this sentiment. I would have assumed there was resentment over immigration laws, resentment that he had been deported, and that he would have viewed his deportation as being mistreated. Instead, he respects that about our country, that we have laws that stand and govern us, and that those laws apply to the poor, the wealthy, and everyone in between. His thoughts gave me even more reason that day to be proud to be American.

CHAPTER FORTY-ONE
BY SALLY

Dark Alley Ways
Callejones Oscuros

THEY WANTED TO take me in to the city to show me around. We hung outside a bit, and they introduced me to neighbors, to some of Luis' friends, and we took photos of everyone to take back to the kids. Flies buzzed in our faces, and the stench still hung in the air. Still, there was a lot of laughter as we walked to the bus stop just around the corner from their building. It was strange to be in what felt like a third world country with dirt, stench, and hopelessness so thick in the air it was hard to breathe, and then see a bus and cars whizzing by.

The bus... ha! What an experience. For some reason, I got such a kick out of it, probably because it represented everything that I love about the Mexican people. It was just so... so... *Mexican!* We jumped onto the bus at the stop. I guess Juan Sr. quickly slipped change in to a teenage kid's hand who was clearly 'in charge,' of who got off and who got on. There was a door at the front and a door at the back of the bus, just like a regular folding school bus door here in the States. This teenager was dressed in jeans and a plain white t-shirt, and wore a backwards cap, tilted to one side. He stood at the bottom step of the back door of the bus, with the door folded open. He hung on, sort of, anyway, with one hand on the door jam, and half of his body, one foot included, dangled out of the bus as it barreled down the road. And he watched. Watched for people at bus stops waiting to be picked up, watched for people giving him a nod that they needed to get off. He watched it all, as the bus driver precariously bobbed and weaved down the streets that were still jammed with the chaos of what seemed to be construction, but looked more like destruction.

When he saw someone waiting at a stop, he beat a certain rhythm on the outside of the bus to signal to the driver to slow down or stop. When the exchange of people had been made, he beat a different rhythm, and the driver would take off again, at high speed. The whole time, the driver, a hugely overweight young guy, drove while cutting up and laughing with his friends who all sat around the front of the bus on buckets, turned upside down in the aisle. The bus was packed, and these kids were totally in charge of it. It ran seamlessly, though they never spoke or even made eye contact that I was aware of.

I was giggling to myself, taking it all in as I stood in the middle of the crowded, small space, clinging to a pole that ran parallel to the roof of the bus so I wouldn't lose my footing as the driver weaved in and out of the mounds of dirt and traffic, through the city that looked like it had never been finished. I wasn't aware, until the translator pointed it out, laughing, that I was drawing a lot of attention. 'I bet you're the only white person that's been on this bus this week.' Juan Sr. piped up, clearly tickled by the translator teasing me. 'Try the only white person all year,' he laughed.

We hopped off the bus near the town square, back to the part of the city close to the border, back to the part that seemed like a border town. We walked around the square, and around the 'shops,' which were really just stands of people selling things, trying to survive. One stand had at least 1,000 cassette tapes. Where did they all come from? Who was going to buy them? How could he possibly feed his family from selling cassette tapes?

As we passed a dark pathway between two buildings, the translator whispered to me, 'Ladies of the evening.' I looked back and realized there were three or four scantily clad women hanging in that pathway. In broad daylight, they were selling their bodies, trying to stay alive. We passed another dark pathway between buildings. And three or four more women, just the same. And another pathway. And more women. It was unreal.

We walked around a while and ended up in the market, Aurora leading me to the best candy to take back to her children, and their favorite tostadas, the ones they had requested, and then they showed me the building where the best food was to eat for lunch. There were several restaurants upstairs, they explained, sort of like what we might compare to a food court at a mall, but not fast food. Juan Sr. wanted to take me to the best one.

The beggars on the bridge as we entered México were hard to see, but they didn't surprise me. I was ready for them. I expected them. The dirt and the poverty were overwhelming, but I knew Juárez would be like that. What met me at the top of these stairs, though, shocked me.

We were chatting about Mexican vanilla as we climbed the huge staircase that split at one level and turned to the right and the left; either side you chose led to the same place. As we climbed a few more stairs, I was so thrown off by what I heard and saw. I had no idea what was happening. About 10 or 15 men and women stood at the top of the stairs, and as soon as we were in view, began yelling, loudly, 'inviting' us to eat at their place. But their actions didn't seem like an invitation; it seemed like an assault. They followed us, almost trying to blockade us into their restaurant. The volume of the yelling, 'Come here! Flautas! Over here! Come eat with us!' was so overwhelming, it took many seconds until I realized what they were doing. I thought something horrible was happening.

The desperation was numbing! Their very livelihood depended on one or two customers a day being split between all of them. I couldn't wrap my head around it. I still can't.

Juan Sr. blessed the meal. We prayed there in that open market restaurant area for several minutes before touching our food. Juan and Alma each called my phone during lunch to speak to their parents. They had another several minutes of prayer on the phone with Juan. Then it was time to go.

They walked us near the border, talking, pointing things out as we went. In the middle of the dirt street, Aurora burst into tears and asked when I would be back. She gave me several individual hugs, asking that I give each away to her children. They gave us messages for each child, all different and all centered on what was going on in their specific lives at the time. We joined hands and prayed one last time, and then my translator and I turned to walk away to go back to the States. Juan and Alma's parents turned to return deeper into the heart of Juárez.

As we took our final steps on Mexican soil, the translator pointed across the street. 'There, that's the only other white person I've seen all day besides you.' I looked across the street to see a haggard, homely man walking in to Juárez from the bridge, quickly, as if on a mission.

'Ah,' said the translator. 'He's a junkie. That's why he's here. For the drugs. And the ladies in the alley ways.'

CHAPTER FORTY-TWO

He is Not the Only "Juan"
El no es el Único Juan

THOUGH JUAN IS an amazing young man who has already overcome so many obstacles and touched many lives, his story is not as unusual as you might think. The most unique, gripping details of his tale are the way he withstood the temptations of the streets and drugs that overtake so many in the inner city and escaped the addiction and anger that loomed in his lineage. The rest of his story, however, is not so unheard of. Living in the midst of the people I grew up with, marrying into the Hispanic as well as the immigrant culture, and teaching English as a second language to immigrants for many years, I have seen Juan's story and those like it from many different angles, over and over again.

But what are we to do? As a Christian in America, what should my opinion be? Certainly there are places in scripture that tell us to be kind to the stranger and the alien. Deuteronomy 10:19 is one of MANY. *And you are to love those who are foreigners, for you were once foreigners in Egypt.* Yet there are just as many scriptures heeding us to live rightly within the law. *Let every person be subject to the governing authorities,* says Romans 13:1, and in 1 Peter, *Be subject to every human institution.* As those who are called to love *and* be blameless, do we as a nation allow illegal immigrants to remain with their families or recognize that America cannot absorb responsibility for other countries and stick to following the law?

As I wrestled with these thoughts, one scripture from Ezekiel 16:49 has continued to tug at my heart: *Now this was the sin of your sister Sodom: She and her daughters were arrogant, overfed, and unconcerned; they did not help the poor and needy.* I remember reading as a child that Sodom was wiped from the face of the Earth because it was detestable in God's sight; I remember imagining what horrible, awful sins the people who lived there must be guilty of. I mean; Lot's wife was turned into a pillar of salt just for turning to look back! It had to be despicable! Later, in a warning to other people who were acting like Sodom, God recounts the sins He saw when He looked at her, arrogance, glutton, and lack of concern. They did not help the poor or the needy.

I do not pretend to have all of the answers. The state of illegal immigration in our country today is the result of decades of migrant workers, loose borders to the south, and a corrupt Mexican government. There is no easy fix. There is not one kind of immigrant, with one kind of circumstance. There is not one political answer that addresses the whole of these issues and secures America while doing it. America grew into this crisis situation over decades; it will not be fixed in a matter of weeks or months, so what do we do in the meantime?

We stand guard that we are not like Sodom. We find those like Juan who cross our path, who may not look like us, act like us, or think like us, and we share life with them. We look out for the poor and the needy, and we speak up for those who cannot speak for themselves. We do not ask for their residency status first.

We love as Jesus would have were He here in the flesh.

We invite them into family, just as God the Father invites us.

I believe it is our job as the Church to be 'Jesus with skin on,' if you will. When Jesus walked on Earth, he ate with unlikely company, went to unlikely places, and kept unlikely friends. He fed them, lived with them, discipled them, and pointed them to God the Father. Certainly, there have been those who walked with Juan like Jesus walked with the lost, inviting him into their homes, into their lives, and into their families, feeding him, teaching him, training him, and loving him. They were not too proud to notice him, not so overfed that they were lazy or greedy. They were moved by compassion and concern. Where would Juan be had they not?

I don't know how to unravel the complicated layers of immigration. I don't know the best way to secure American borders in such a tumultuous time in the world or how to rightly solve or unite decades of families that have crossed borders illegally and separated themselves. I pray for immigration reform that is inspired by God, protects this country that I love, and provides true paths to citizenship for those honest, hardworking men and women who love what America stands for and would take advantage of every opportunity they are offered.

In the meantime, I pray that I won't be arrogant, overfed, or unconcerned. I pray that I won't be like Sodom.

CHAPTER FORTY-THREE
BY JUAN

Today
Hoy

TODAY, I WOKE UP far from Juárez; far from my parents, from Nena, from my nieces and nephews. Far from the dirt, loud music, and corruption that filled the air of my early childhood. I woke up far from fear and far from alley ways lined with desperation and pain. I woke up at home in my apartment at the YWAM base in East Dallas and got ready for work. I woke my brothers, Luis and Isaac—who live with me in the United States now—and told them to get ready for school.

Today, I am at peace. I am not angry. I am not addicted. I am not hungry or homeless. Today, I have an Associate's degree, and I have a job. I am deeply involved in Youth With a Mission ministries in Dallas, serving the youth and the leadership. I am part of that leadership. My apartment is now the hub, much like Ralph's used to be, for teenagers; whether they come because they are a part of YWAM ministries, or they come home with Luis and Isaac from school, I get to hang out with them, share with them, build relationships with them, and minister to them. I get to talk to them about all sorts of things, and I get to point them toward my God.

Today, I have Jesus. I am dumbfounded He has seen fit to spare me from adversity. Today, I should be a perfect number on a page filled with statistics of gang violence, poverty, drug use, dropouts, minority male incarceration, or premature death. I am not supposed to be here, today, but I am.

Today, I woke in the astounding privilege of God's presence. His peace. There is still distress and deep sadness in the separation from my family, but I have someone to come home to. I am not alone anymore; He is here with me. I don't have to wander the streets, up and down sidewalks, being tempted by overpasses that could help me end the pain, looking for shelter. He is my place to rest. Today, I don't have to figure out the next step alone. I have family. I have a refuge. Today, I have hope.

I have been trained up, educated, and given opportunities to learn, to lead, and to be loved by a spiritual family that has adopted me. I have a long list of people who call me their own. Besides Pastor Clay, David Funke, and Dustin Sample, Scott Robson has led me, taught me, loved me, and fathered me in so many ways. He has provided for me spiritually, emotionally, and financially over the years. Brian and Carolyn Strickfaden, another family from Trinity Church Dallas, have taken me in as theirs. They have loved me as if I was their own son and have been instrumental in helping me take care of my brothers since their arrival in the States. They have vouched for me to others in a way that has led to jobs, training, and resources. They have fed my brothers and I countless meals over countless tables, always asking how we were or what we needed and filling every hole in our lives they possibly could. I cannot begin to list everyone who has filled my life these past years, brought me in to their family, loved me, and poured in to me. All I can say is that I am truly humbled to be loved by such wonderful people.

My heart's desire now is to turn and do these things for the next generation, to minister in the same ways I have been ministered to for years. My dream would be for God to open doors for me to minister through music because it has had such a powerful, lasting, continual

Brian & Carolyn Strickfaden with Juan and Amy Mulloy.

impact on my life that I want to see spread. I want to be used in a way that will turn the "hearts of the fathers back to the children and the hearts of the children back to their fathers," (Malachi 4:6). Whatever God has planned for me, I trust him today.

I trust Him to continue to teach me what it is to be a man—to continue to show me that manhood is not about age, but about responsibility and character. Today, it is a struggle to play the role of father to my two younger brothers at such a young age and with such limited examples of what it is to be a good father, but I know God has placed people in my life to show me the way real men cling to Him and are molded by Him. Today, I ask the Lord to make me more like Jesus.

Today, I can work legally under my temporary status provided by the Deferred Action for Childhood Arrivals (DACA). I am pursuing paths to residency and citizenship because America is my home, the only home I've ever known. I am aware that immigration is a very touchy topic politically, and I know I don't understand everything that makes it complicated. I know America must be protected, and that it's not fair when people don't follow the law, but I also know there are many, many in this country just like me. They were brought to America by parents at such a young age that their history is tied more to this land than any other; they only want the chance to prove themselves, use their talents, and lead fulfilling lives. Today, I pray for a solution that is good for America, but does not turn its back on youth who had no choice in the matter of their residency and have no other home but here.

Today, I have expectation. I don't know when or how it will be, but I am certain I will see my parents again soon. This is a dream I cling to. It's a dream I've had ever since my parents left. You know what? I'm glad they did. God was intimately aware of what I needed, and there was not one day He did not see me or tend to me. Had my parents stayed, I'm sure I would have followed in my father's rough path. I would not have had to lean into the Lord or lean into other people. My heart would have hardened; anger would have been fed and given way to rage. Mediocrity would have led me to drop out, and I have no doubt the streets would have claimed my life.

Today, my parents are clean and drug free. Today, they have found God again and have climbed back into His loving arms. Though they struggle in Juárez, they cling to the Lord. Had things gone differently, they would not have received or responded to a wakeup call. My father would probably be dead. My family would have been ripped apart in other ways. My life has not been easy on the surface, but I'm not so sure that our Heavenly Father is always concerned with our earthly ease and comfort. I feel that He is concerned with eternity. Today, my eternity and the eternal futures of my family are secure.

Today, I have walked the road out of Juárez. I have crossed bridges, first in those cowboy boots I used to trudge around in when I was a little boy, and across borders, through dirt and snow. Those roads and bridges, have brought me here to America, to freedom. Today, I have not simply been left in America or left *to* America. I have been left in the hands of Jesus, and He has saved my life.

Juan's high school graduation, North Dallas High School, 2008, with Carl Trevino and Rafael (Ralph) Rivera.

The men living at the Dallas YWAM housing. Top Row: Ofa, Juan, David, Luis, Miles. Bottom Row: Wilson, Jose, Richie.

The Left in America (LiA) Organization

Left in America Organization (LIA) is a Texas Non-Profit Organization. LIA's work began in 2012 and was officially formed as a Texas Non-Profit Organization in 2013 with the initial purpose of writing and publishing the story of Juan Terrazas. LIA will continue to promote and distribute the book *Left in America*, support the ministry of Juan Terrazas, and support the work of YWAM Dallas.

LIA is a non-denomination, Christian Organization. Individuals and organizations who wish to become members of LIA can do so by contacting one of the Directors of LIA or by sending a request to the organization at the address below.

For the purpose of writing the book, *Left in America*, LIA has received contributions for expenses and operations. All funds raised to date are used solely for that function.

Individuals and organizations that would like to contribute to the Left In America Organization can do so by sending contributions to:

Left in America Organization
154 Glass St., Suite 108
Dallas, TX 75207

LIA does encourage churches, organizations, and individuals to become involved in supporting the work of organizations and individuals who care for and support children of illegal immigrations who have been left in America. We hope that you not only support these organizations financially, but also by praying and by volunteering your time and efforts.

To get involved, please contact us at www.leftinamerica.org.

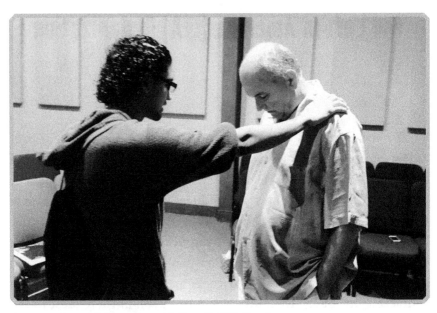

Juan praying with June Jones, College & NFL Coach, 2014

Matthew 25: 31–45

When the Son of Man comes in his glory, and all the angels with him, he will sit on his glorious throne. All the nations will be gathered before him, and he will separate the people one from another as a shepherd separates the sheep from the goats. He will put the sheep on his right and the goats on his left.

Then the King will say to those on his right, "Come, you who are blessed by my Father; take your inheritance, the kingdom prepared for you since the creation of the world. For I was hungry and you gave me something to eat, I was thirsty and you gave me something to drink, I was a stranger and you invited me in, I needed clothes and you clothed me, I was sick and you looked after me, I was in prison and you came to visit me."

Then the righteous will answer him, "Lord, when did we see you hungry and feed you, or thirst and give you something to drink? When did we see you a stranger and invite you in, or needing clothes and clothe you? When did we see you sick or in prison and go to visit you?"

The King will reply, "Truly I tell you, whatever you did for one of the least of these brothers and sisters of mine, you did for me."

Then he will say to those on his left, "Depart from me, you who are cursed, into the eternal fire prepared for the devil and his angels. For I was hungry and you gave me nothing to eat, I was thirsty and you gave me nothing to drink, and I was a stranger and you did not invite me in, I needed clothes and you did not clothe me, I was sick and in prison and you did not look after me."

They also will answer, "Lord, when did we see you hungry or thirsty or a stranger or needing clothes or sick or in prison, and did not help you?" "He will reply, 'Truly I tell you, whatever you did not do for one of the least of these, you did not do for me'."

Juan's Quotes & Poems

April 24, 2008

Things in life come unexpected. Sometimes, we don't know what to do when we feel stuck in a world of devastation. This is how I felt a while back ago; it wasn't pretty, but I'm over it now. I know if my mind is set to be ambitious, sustaining on pursuing my goal, I know what I am capable of. Undermining the situation will not help it get better because it comes right back diminishing you. Feeling like this didn't kill me; it only made me stronger!

"How I Feel!" written Senior Year

Where will my next step take me

Where will I end up, where will I be

What do I have to do to get out of this terrible scene

Why can't life be the way it was before, when it wasn't such a painful sore

Can somebody help me, show me a way to escape

How can I get away, it's something I can't ignore

It's difficult to get away, don't know how to continue, should I keep going or stay

Many times I don't know what to do, where to go, how to feel, or even what to say

I feel all alone in a cloudy, thundery storm,

I may seem optimistic on the outside but in reality inside I'm broken, so torn

It's so difficult, I'm being held hostage, I'm suffocating

being alone in a world like this is devastating

I wonder how much longer will it last, should I continue on fighting

I'm trying but the negative keeps on surrounding

I hate this, I want to get away, I feel like crying

It kills me inside, I feel like dying

I try to escape, the adversaries I try to undermined

I am running out of space to move, I fell shortly timed

What can I do, what should I do

Should I keep going, with myself should I proceed

Can somebody please hear me, help me? I want to be free...

October 29, 2009

I pray You bring me Joy, bring me Peace, bring the chance to be free, bring me any that bring you Glory. I know there will be days when this life brings me pain, but if that's what it takes to praise You, then, Jesus, bring the rain!

October 17, 2010

I just got that 2020 vision. I'm really excited to see all that is going to happen within the next decade. I'm tired of hearing "let's see things happen" but nothing ever happens. How about we make things happen? I'm looking for people who are willing to go on the ride and change this world for Christ, real talk. You in?

November 27, 2011

"Knowing You, Jesus, Knowing You, there is no greater thing. You're my all, You're the best, You're my joy, my righteousness, and I love You, Lord."

September 16, 2012

This is crazy, but I feel as if I've fallen in love with the Lord for the first time. I cannot explain what happened, but I know without a doubt He hears my cries and has walked every step with me. Seven years ago, I did not know He would have orchestrated everything that has happened to my family for our good. It amazes my heart to have someone who truly cares and loves without any fault.

I say this because my hope and prayer is that He will draw you near to Him, and you surrender your heart to Him. When Jesus is at the center of it all, nothing else matters...

September 17, 2012

I see today as one of the most special days ever. With that said, I want to wish my precious baby sister, Alma, a great happy birthday! You are a strong blessing and awesome young lady. I love and believe in you, and I know you will go far in life despite anything that comes your way. Remember that you're not alone, and we are in this together. I am blessed to have you in my life. I love you!!! PS: You're still a dufus, and I'm glad I'm related to you (:

October 8, 2012

If following the Lord Jesus, in the eyes if the world means I'm a loser, then I'll take the "L."

October 19, 2012

Every one of us has God given gifts and talents, and there is nothing more frustrating than to see people waste their lives searching for other things. Ask the Lord what He has called you to, and when He tells you, pursue it with your whole heart because only then will you find true satisfaction, in doing Christ's purpose in your life. Do not let your talents go to waste because it will sound disappointing to say years from now, "Oh, I wish I could have done this or that."

The unhappy people are those who are not fulfilling their purposes. There is greatness and so much more in us than we can ever imagine. This is coming from someone who never thought of himself to have any creativity or great gifts. Hear me out, and I pray you lose yourself in Christ to find who you truly are.

October 28, 2012

People think being a Christian is boring because all they see is a bunch of rules and regulations. They think it's boring, and we have no life. Well, they obviously don't know my God, and the freedom He has purchased and what He does to a human heart.

October 28, 2012 via Instagram

Hello Dallas, you've been my home since I was a child. Despite how many odds came against me, I learned to persevere. I learned not to back down, even now. I'm living for the day the Lord uses me to bring you back to Him.

June 16, 2013

Dad,

When I was child, you didn't let me run while, but we used to race, you'd let me win/ called me champion/ I'm even tatted on your skin/ you weren't the greatest, but you're my best mess/ I'm blessed you pressed/ with troubles you dealt, and trauma you felt trying to bring support/ feeling inadequate without a job of some sort/ later deported, chaos, distort/ Dad, I cried that night/ tried to stay strong but couldn't hold the song/ I sit back and think, your words I heard, whether sober or drunk/ deep down they sunk/ "Be someone in life"/ thanks to your effort, labor, I found more, I'm a child of Christ, together we'll rise... I miss you; I can't wait to see you, feel your touch, feel your embrace, and see your face...

July 25, 2013

We just had an awesome time ministering at The Rock! We did "The House is on Fire Skit." Kat, Jade, and Richie shared testimonies, and Jade got to dance. I got to rap, share my testimony and a message. I appreciate the prayers because we have seen the Lord move on this trip.

August 26, 2013

Five years ago this week, I am reminded of the night I lay near a small closet room at a friend's apartment crying out to God saying, "God I'm tired of living life my own way. I'm tired of going from house to house and place to place, not knowing if I'm going to have food to eat or a place to stay; or if I will ever be able to talk to my parents again. I don't want to go my own way anymore; I surrender in Jesus' name.." The next day I felt a voice in my spirit clearly, as if someone saying to me, "Do not worry about it son, but lay it all down to me; and follow my path." Everything that has happened to me these past five years, words cannot convey. All I ever truly wanted was to be loved and to love. All I ever hoped and dreamed is no longer a dream, but reality.

September 17, 2013

The only way for you to ever find out if something is possible is to give it a try. If you never allow yourself to try new things, you will never know exactly what you missed out on. Every time you aim for nothing, you will always hit it; every shot not taken is a missed shot. What do you have to lose: your shame, doubt, guilt, fear, etc...

October 29, 2013

"There has to be so much more to life than what I see" is the very thought that continually resounded in my heart and mind growing up as a teenager, and the Lord used that to draw me nigh unto Him. You could do so much in life, but if you never get to know Jesus, life is pointless.

November 7, 2013

Statistically, it was said that I'd be found hitting up a lick in the streets hustling/ never should have been a high school graduate or been to college/ should've had confirming imprints in my brain/ knowing it was common choosing the easy lane/ only to drink up to ease my pain/ I had hard knocks on my soul, "saying, like them, you're not the same"/ as a "tough man" pretense/ I was a damsel in distress/ I ain't even supposed to be here/ I'm supposed to be nothing/ but there's so much more to "Life" and that "More" made me something.

December 30, 2013

In other news besides the Cowboy's losing, my sister Alma came over to give my brother Luis a phone for Christmas as a surprise, but little did she know she would be surprised herself by seeing our baby brother Isaac, whom we had not seen since he was four years old. It has been about 9 years that we have been split up because of my dad's deportation. Being separated has knitted us closer than anything ever would have. I give gory to the Lord Jesus for the grace and mercy He has bestowed upon our family.

"Been separated many years, but united as One with a river made of tears."

January 17, 2014

My heart was blessed earlier today at YWAM Dallas' Kid's Club. One of the little girls was like, "Mr., Mr! I have something to share with you, but I have to sing it to you first!"

"Ok, what is it?"

"I heard this song on the Internet, and I want to share it with you."

"Ok, which one is it?"

She started to say the hook to my "Victory" song "I can see it, I can hear it, I can smell it, I can taste it, I can feel it when I'm reaching, I walk in Victory!"

She continued to sing the first verse. "If God be for us, who can be against us, that's the truth that I trust, from the King Jesus."

Out of the past few years I've been working with music, I have not been as blessed as I have tonight after hearing Melanie, who is about 12 years old, at YWAM Dalllas. I know there is a purpose on why I believe the Lord called me to rap; I'm starting to see more of its impact on this children.

January 19, 2014

In retrospect, I reminisce all that has occurred in my life. Even until this very moment. I do not accredit myself to be any better or less in comparison to anyone due to my struggles and victories. Each person has a different situation, some overcome, and some are overtaken. I hope you overcome.

As most of you know my testimony, I didn't ask to be left without my parents at the age of 14, to be kicked out at 15, and start house hopping in hope to find a family to fit in. I was placed in this predicament without a choice. I know life comes at us with difficulties, and things may get worse before they get any better. My heart goes out to those who are faced with a heavy yoke. You weren't meant to carry that because I know there is rest for the weary. Listen to this mystery, the Lord looks upon the broken and contrite heart, If you are the kind of person that wants to stay "strong" and not shed a tear, that's foolish because you will only build bitterness and pride within yourself; cry out to Him tonight that His ear will be attentive to you. I walked and will walk through the fire, yet, I will not be burnt or even smell like smoke, for He is with me. The waters may rise upon me, yet, I will not drown, for He is with me. Something happened inside of my heart that changed my paradigm, and my hope and prayer is that such thing will happen to you, even at a greater measure.

February 1, 2014

I wasn't favored to make it,
But He stepped in and saved me,
He cared about the immigrant,
It's evident He's intimate,
He's into me like cinnamon,
The world will know imminent,
He's infinite, omnipotent,
On top of things like sovereign,
He puts the lonely in families,
He put me in a family,
Yeah, and Lord, I pray You take all of me.

March 2, 2014

This is to all the ladies out there. I made this song specifically for women due to my experience of seeing many mistreated and seeing many allow themselves to be mistreated. You don't have to live that way. On behalf of several men who have repented, I apologize to the women for looking at them as a tool or piece of meat. You are worth so much more than to be treated in such way. You probably never had a real father to show you were a princess.

I hope this song helps you see there is healing for you pain; I hope you see the God that saved me. If you are hurting in any way or know of any woman hurting from any male figure that did them wrong, there is only one man that can heal your heart. He can take the broken pieces of your heart and put them back together better than before if you believe on Him and let Him. Don't ever let a man put a price on you, but look to the Lord Jesus. How will you ever find your purpose if you never look to Him by whom you were created? If you open your heart and listen, He's saying, "You're beautiful, specifically made, unique in all the way you're shaped, Apple of His Eye, Star in the Sky." Therefore you can say, "I'm beautiful, specifically made, unique in all the way I'm shaped, Apple of His Eye, Star in the Sky."

March 4, 2014

Though my troubles compass me about and be many, I will lay me down in peace, for the Lord sustains me and makes me dwell in safety. His peace that surpasses all understanding is the song in my heart...

April 7, 2014

"We exalt your name high above the heavens.. All of creation sings praise praise."

I live to see this day come to pass. My heart's desire is the hope that you will see Him. The only way to see is in faith; other than that, you will never taste and see Him. Something happened on the inside of my heart as I cried out to the Lord in that small closet room several years ago. I've never been the same since. I hope your heart cries out the exact words mine did, "God I'm tired of living life my own my. I don't want to do things my own way anymore. I surrender, in Jesus' name; I give you my heart." Today is your day...

April 23, 2014

I don't claim to know it all or have it all held together, but I know the One who knows it all and by whom I'm held together. Just as the world is held by the Cross, He's the laminin* to my body.

---

* **Laminins** are high-molecular proteins that are a major component of the network foundation for most cells and organs, basically holding our body together.

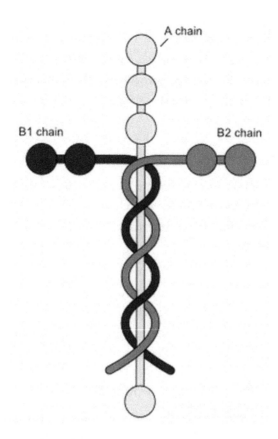

For by Him all things were created that are in heaven and that are on earth, visible and invisible, whether thrones or dominions or principalities or powers. All things were created through Him and for Him. And He is before all things, and in Him all things consist.

Colossians 1:16-17

April 26, 2014

The Lord created the Heavens and the Earth and everything they contain. The skies, the seas and their vastness were made by Him, and there is not one thing that was not created by Him;, yet, all came into existence by His Word; He spoke it. Out of all things He created, the most beautiful is the Cross, by which the world is held together.

April 29, 2014

People never truly fall in love; rather, fools only fall in pits. True love is only known to grow with the person you are with. Never make decisions based on feelings; but, he who seeks counsel is wise.

May 3, 2014

I am known of Him, for He calls me by name. As a father has pity on his son, so has He looked on me with love.
I am crowned with loving kindness and tender mercies. I will not forget His promises.

May 13, 2014

A man is most strong when he is weak. A man is most lifted high when he is humbled. A man is most powerful when he is meek.
A boy becomes a man when he comes to realize it's not about him.

Crack in his wall after a thunderstorm, shape of heart, in Juan's diary May 14th Facebook posting.

May 14, 2014

Even during thunderstorms in Dallas, I find little guys like this. When the storm rains down on me, "His peace surpassing understanding is a song in my heart."

May 17, 2014

I am crowned with lovingkindness and tender mercies. It is for His compassions that fail not, for His mercies that are afresh I am not consumed this day. He is righteous in all His ways and holy in all His works. I look deep into His eyes, and He burns with love for me. There is no love greater. He knows me; He calls me by name. This day shall I rejoice henceforth.

May 18, 2014

The greatest act of love is preferring someone else before yourself and putting their needs above yours. It's even as simple as seeing my baby brother give the last piece of pizza to his friend when he knew it was the last one in the box. I was reminded of why I'm here.

May 18, 2014

What is hope to a man that can be seen, for hope that can be seen is no hope at all. Hope in which I hope is the evidence of what I have not seen, for I earnestly await rest for my soul. Our momentary struggles have no comparison to the eternal glory we will gain. I hope in Thee: awake my soul. Make haste; tarry not.

May 21, 2014

"You know my longing, and You hear my every thought and prayer. You are my refuge, the One that I run to. I find my strength in You alone... I live my life for one thing, poured out as an offering, an offering of worship, I give to you now."

May 22, 2014

He crowns me with loving kindness and tender mercies.

May 24, 2014

This one thing I know, only the Lord is the One to fulfill the desire of the heart, and I, as the man, long to take my part in the fill.

Juan and his girlfriend, Amy Mulloy

May 26, 2014 via Instagram

Things easily handed down to you are scarcely appreciated, yet true value is found in those things you had to fight for.

May 29, 2014

I do not know the end result to my all, but this one thing I grow in confidence, in that I know You, the One who holds the end result to my all.

June 3, 2014

(At work) «Hey Smooth, come here real quick.» I'm not about to lie, that's actually a cool nickname. My boy Ricardo told me that might be God saying that things were probably going to go a little smoother for me. I really can't tell you how many nicknames I have now. They just keep coming.

June 4, 2014

I will not forget Your promises; I will not forget that nothing is impossible; I will not forget Your Love.

September 13, 2014

People have said that I don't belong here because I'm an outsider. I know what it's like to be an immigrant.

October 17, 2014 · Got Engaged to Amy Mulloy

A year ago on October 20th, I met this beautiful young lady that I had ever laid eyes on, and I could not stop thinking about her. A few months later, I told her I was interested in her, and I have thoroughly enjoyed getting to know her. I have been blessed, more than I could have ever imagined being with her. She has inspired and encouraged me to draw closer to the Lord like no other person has. The Lord blessed the broken road that led me straight her. The best is yet to come, Amy, and I love you!

Juan and his fiancé, Amy Mulloy

November 12, 2014

Though my troubles compass me about and be many, I will lay me down in peace, for the Lord sustains me and makes me dwell in safety. His peace that surpasses all understanding is the song in my heart...

December 28, 2014

Life is full of adventures, yet, life is nothing if you have no one to walk alongside you.

Eyes Begin to Tear Up

You see your child being highly afflicted!

Take heed to his words, I know you hear all the prayers he has lifted,
However, little by little, to his adversaries, he is being distributed,
Physically and spiritually he begins to grow weary,

Look on him and deliver him from his adversary,

This one thing he asks, "Cover me not with a facial mask but with your presence that will last."

His eyes begin to tear up as the thought of the impossible comes about,

The clouds gather dark, and the world soon blacks out, the waves of his life rage in a manner so drastic,

I see him, where can he go when his movement is forcefully limited? It sometimes kills him inside having to take this ride,

Yet, there are many reasons he remains alive,

His eyes are kept looking forward ahead, but he continues to stumble side to side,

He wonders? When will he see them by whom he was conceived? A cry of his heart is to at least have a quick glance,

Year after year he cries a loud cry, his eyes have become dry, many rivers stream down beneath his feet,

They flow to the seas where they have become very deep, tear after tear has been sowed, what and when will he reap? You've seen him and how he has gone through the fire,

Thus You say, "I've always held on to you and every tear you've cried, I've held in a bottle made of sapphire,

I've made you into a man of endurance, love, strength and persistence, your tears to me, they shine,

And I will continue to pour out my Love on you so divine, come, you will find all you need as you seek me,

I hear your petitions and see when your eyes, once again, go teary..."

"Someone to come Home to"

In retrospect, I reminisce my December being filled with lonesome nights, and I had no one to come home to. I wish there were things I could have done to belong, but who was there for me to come home to? "I wish I didn't feel this way; 'This is my December,' so I thought. I battled with depressing thoughts that talked. From my waking in the morning, to the laying of my head, I shed tears as I lay in bed, and at times, I wished to be dead. Was there someone to come home to? I had many in my sight; yet, there was none to warmth my heart. Torn apart, neglected at heart, and thrown as a dart missing the mark. "Come home," was there such to believe when all was but a naught? Tied as a knot and liberty I besought; however, freedom came not in whatever I sought. Tear after tear I sowed in hope one day love I would know, if there was such to unfold. My ears tingled for any utterance, unto me, untold. I searched and beseeched, as I desired for any love to come unto me unleashed. I longed with passion for strong affection to bestow my adoration on another person. Though, I acted and spoke out in hope to be paid attention, all I desired was to let love flow and not be inattention; such was my intention. My heart's pursuit has been to find a loving host to hold close and know I love the most. Yet, who was I to come home to? "Come home," was there such to believe when I saw naught? I besought and sought, until one day, an utterance tingled in my ears, which transfigured my paradigm and brought unto me cheers; He said unto me, "You have someone to come home to." Now I know; "I have someone to come home to; I have someone to come home to."

PICTURES OF JUAN THROUGH THE YEARS

Juan after a long weekend at Dallas Metro Kidz Camp, 2005.

Richie and Juan in San Antonio with Dallas Metro, 2006.

Juan's High School Prom, 2008.

Juan at North Park
Mall, Dallas, TX,
2010.

Juan and El Centro College friends, 2010.

PICTURES
OF JUAN
WORKING
WITH
MISSION
GROUPS

Juan working with YWAM children, 2013.

Juan translating for David Funke for the Parents at the YWAM Christmas program in 2011.

Juan working with David Funke, helping a group of Karen refugees from Burma, at YWAM Tyler base camp.

Juan and David, with Karen refugees, 2008.

Juan working with a kid at Metro Summer Camp 2009.

Juan clowning around with children, Dallas Metro Camp, 2011.

Barbara Wallace and Juan at Dallas Metro Camp, 2011.

Juan and his friend Jessie at Dallas Metro Summer Camp, 2011.

Roman, Juan, Jesus, & Jessie at Dallas Metro Summer Camp, 2008.

Jonas, Jessie, Juan, Timothy, and Ricky at Summer Camp, 2009.

Juan working with children, 2011.

FINAL THOUGHTS

"Children happen to be born into a situation that is beyond
their control."

—*Gloria Campos*, retired Evening Host
WFAA (ABC) News, Dallas

Today, America has over 300,000 illegal children who have
been brought to America before they were 16 years old.
Many of the parents of these children were forced to leave
America, but left their children here.
As a Christian, what do you think Jesus would want you to
do for these children?

Left in America Organization
154 Glass St., Suite 108
Dallas, TX 75207
www.leftinamerica.org

The pastor who married Juan's parents on May 14, 1996, Jim Paul, also married Juan and Amy Mulloy on June 14, 2015 at the Robert Carr Chapel on the TCU Campus in Fort Worth, Texas. Mr. & Mrs. Terrazas currently reside in Atlanta, Georgia.

Moving out of Dallas to Atlanta has been a step of faith in trusting the Lord, believing He has called me out of my comfort zone. Moving to a new city, in my eyes, is not starting over, but it is a continual building on to the foundation that has been laid in my life. I enjoy music, and I see the great impact it has in people's lives. Since I was fifteen years old, I have felt the call to reach out to the lost, broken, and hopeless through music, but I did not know how to go about it until I surrendered my heart to the Lord. My heart's desire is to reach out to people's hearts and give them the Hope of Life that was given to me in the name of Jesus. For the future, I hope to be involved in full-time ministry and music. However, above my ministry, I am called to be a husband to my wife, so I look forward in growing and maturing to learn how to be the best man I can for Amy. In everything I do, I hope to lead people to know the name of the Lord because His promise in Psalm 9:10 is that for those who know His name will put their trust in Him, and He never forsakes those who seek Him.

To contact Juan personally, his email is *jterrazas@leftinamerica.org*